3/92

NM 6³⁵

D1578060

HIKING TRAILS
OF THE SANDIA AND MANZANO MOUNTAINS
Including Cross-Country Ski Information

by Kay Matthews

Heritage Associates, Inc.
P.O. Box 6291
Albuquerque, New Mexico 87197

Copyright © 1984 by Kay Matthews
All rights reserved, including those to reproduce this book,
or parts thereof, in any form, without permission in writing
from the Publisher.

First Edition
Second Printing, 1986

Designed by Lisa D. Madsen

Cover photograph by Stephen G. Maurer

ISBN 0-910467-02-1
Library of Congress Catalog Card No.: 84-62359

CONTENTS

INTRODUCTION

PART I. GENERAL INFORMATION

PART II. HIKING TRAILS IN THE SANDIA MOUNTAINS

ii

PART III.
HIKING TRAILS IN THE MANZANO MOUNTAINS

PART IV.
CROSS-COUNTRY SKI TRAILS
IN THE SANDIA MOUNTAINS

PART V.
CROSS-COUNTRY SKI TRAILS
IN THE MANZANO MOUNTAINS

Acknowledgments

I would like to thank my Forest Service friends—Jackie, Marty, John, Bill, Dennis, and Keith—for their assistance and information. Thanks, also, to my hiking and skiing buddies, Mark and Jakob.

INTRODUCTION

Ten million years ago, just east of where the Rio Grande now flows, a mountain chain was formed, like a trapdoor lifting from the floor, exposing a 20,000-foot rock face to the west and gentler, sloping canyons to the east. During these millions of years the mountains have eroded, layering the Rio Grande valley with sediment into which water drained and was held in an underground reservoir. Thus, the mountains provided a vast water supply for the city that was eventually built at their base. Today, the Sandia Mountains, at half their original height, rise 10,680 feet above sea level and a full mile above Albuquerque, the city using that great underground lake.

The Sandias are sometimes referred to as Albuquerque's playground, accessible as one's own back yard. But that description seems to lack reverence for the mountains' ancient history, for their stature in the scheme of things. Perhaps it originated with people who had little experience of the mountains—who had never hiked the trails, climbed the granite rocks, or sat still by the springs and sensed a world separate from our own. The only exposure that many people ever have to the Sandias is an automobile ride to the Crest, a trip up the Tramway, or an afternoon in a crowded picnic ground. These are all legitimate, enjoyable activities, but the word "enjoy" suggests a limited experience, a "playground" concept. The Sandias offer us much more than a playground; they give us the opportunity to appreciate the grandeur of the natural world untouched by human hands. To this world we have a moral responsibility—to ensure that the mountains' use does not become abuse, that they be preserved to support an intricate life system in which we are visitors only.

This book is a guide for responsible users, the hikers who periodically want to escape from our civilized world, who want to use their feet and lungs and muscles to relate at first hand to a natural environment. Practically, it details the trail systems, providing information for well-planned hikes with descriptions of trail heads, trail lengths, elevations, degrees of difficulty, trail conditions, interesting formations, flora, and fauna. Philosophically, this guide encourages people to come to know a mountain in all its splendid detail, for such knowledge enhances our sense of place and purpose in the world.

Albuquerque hikers need not limit their experience to the Sandias. Also accessible for day hikes is the Manzano mountain range, running south for forty miles from Tijeras Canyon to Mountainair. The Manzanos, geographically similar to the Sandias, also offer extensive trail systems and a bounty of all that constitutes wilderness: rugged terrain, expansive vistas, high mountain meadows, and diverse vegetation and wildlife. And because they are not as close to the city as the Sandias, they provide even more opportunity for solitude and wilderness hiking. You will share this remoteness with the bear and the mountain lion, at home in these wild surroundings. I wish to encourage my readers to explore the Manzanos not only for wilderness experience, but also to help reduce the people-impact upon the Sandias.

PART I.
GENERAL INFORMATION

Management

The Sandia Mountains are managed as part of the National Forest system, specifically by the Sandia Ranger District of the Cibola National Forest. Recreation is the primary concern of the management; no timbering or range permits are issued, and although some mining leases remain extant, there is virtually no mining activity.

The Sandia District is small—115,000 acres—compared to others in the forest system, but it is busy due to its proximity to Albuquerque. As the city has grown, so have the developed recreational facilities in the mountains: fourteen picnic areas, the Sandia Crest Highway ending at a restaurant and gift shop, the Sandia Peak Tramway and Ski Area, fourteen maintained hiking trails, the Cienega Nature Trail for the Handicapped, and the Snowplay Area.

To protect mountain resources, several mandates restrict certain people uses. In 1921, 67,000 acres of the Sandias were declared a game refuge, and hunting with firearms was prohibited. There is an annual bow season for deer, however. In 1978, 38,000 acres were incorporated into the National Wilderness system as "an area of Federal land retaining its primeval character and influence, without permanent improvements or habitation, which is protected and managed so as to preserve its natural condition . . . ." This wilderness classification ensures against any further development in the Sandias within the wilderness boundary and provides additional "primitive" recreation in conjunction with the developed recreational sites outside the boundary. Most of the trails described in this book are in the Sandia Mountain Wilderness.

In 1982 the Forest Service finally acquired a 7,000-acre tract of land called the Elena Gallegos Land Grant, contiguous to the wilderness but under the trusteeship of the Albuquerque Academy. Through a trade of other federal lands, and with the help of the city of Albuquerque, the Forest Service incorporated this land into the wilderness system, where it truly belongs. It runs east from Tramway Boulevard up to the Crest and south from the Tramway to Embudito Canyon.

The Manzano Mountains are managed for multiple use by the Mountainair Ranger District. This use includes recreation, and both timber and range permits are issued. Part of the Manzanos was also designated as wilderness in 1978; the 37,000-acre Manzano Mountain Wilderness, more isolated and less traveled than the Sandia Wilderness, provides for an even more "primitive" recreation. The Manzano trails described here are mostly within the wilderness area.

Geology

The Sandias extend southeast to northwest for twenty-two miles from Tijeras Canyon to Placitas. The western boundary is the Albuquerque basin; the eastern boundary, approximately 12 miles away, is harder to distinguish because of its more gentle slope. The eastern tilt and the steeper western exposure are the result of the tilted fault block uplift which created the Sandias. About ten million years ago the fault began to form along the north-south Rio Grande Rift; the rough west side of the mountains is the face of the rupture while the sloping east side is the top of the tilted block. Scientists estimate that the original height of the uplifted mountains exceeded 20,000 feet above sea level.

The west face of the Sandias exposes the kinds of rock that make up the mountains. Precambrian granite, approximately 1.5 billion years old, comprises the greater part of the mountains; it was formed deep within the earth, the result of cooling magma. This granite, an aggregate of various minerals—feldspar, quartz, and mica—fractured into blocks of rock of all shapes and sizes; hence the canyons, boulders, knobs, spires, and peaks which form the west face.

After the granite cooled in the earth's crust, a billion years passed while it was slowly exposed and then submerged in the seas of the early Paleozoic era. These seas laid down the layers of sedimentary rock which form the rim of the Sandias. Where the sedimentary rocks make contact with the Sandia Granite is known as the Great Unconformity. The layers of rock which lie directly on the granite are in the Magdalena Group of the Pennsylvanian epoch, which occurred in middle Paleozoic time. The Magdalena is about 300 million years old; made up of the Sandia and Madera Formations, it forms the several-hundred feet of shale, limestone, and lighter-colored sandstone strata which are the capping rim of the Sandias. Ocean fossils can be found in this layered rock, especially along the upper La Luz and Crest Spur trails.

The Manzanos, like the Sandias, are a long, narrow range running basically north and south from the eastern end of the Isleta Indian Reservation to U.S. Highway 60. They rise from a 6,000-foot elevation in the foothills to 10,098 feet at Manzano Peak. Also formed by a tilted fault block, the east and west sides resemble the Sandias: rugged, craggy canyons above the Rio

Grande valley to the west and gentle, timbered slopes rising from the Estancia valley to the east.

Weather and Life Zones

Although over 10,000 feet of the Sandias is thought to have eroded down their western face, there is still a 5,000-foot elevational difference between Albuquerque and the Sandia Crest and a corresponding difference in climate. Between city and mountaintop occur four of the seven climate, or life, zones, each with its own characteristic vegetation.

In the foothills near Albuquerque, juniper and piñon are familiar landmarks. In this Upper Sonoran life zone, from 6,500 to 7,600 feet, grow the favorite chamisa and the Apache plume; hardwood cottonwoods and box elders usually denote a water source. There are many mountain springs in this zone, but due to heat of summer or lack of winter snow, they dry up quickly. Trails in the Upper Sonoran can be very hot for hiking, even when the temperature at the Crest is considerably cooler.

From 7,600 to 8,200 feet is the Transition zone, where the piñon-juniper population gradually gives way to Gambel oak and ponderosa pine. An occasional limber pine or aspen indicates the beginnings of the next highest zone, the Canadian. Here grow the Douglas fir, white fir, aspen, and Rocky Mountain maple. The highest zone found in the Sandias is called the Hudsonian, above 10,000 feet. Engelmann spruce, Douglas fir, corkbark fir, and limber pine create the densest, most homogenous type of growth on the mountains.

The climatic conditions which determine the different vegetation in each zone are temperature and precipitation. The Canadian and Hudsonian zones are the coolest and moistest; the average rainfall at Sandia Crest is 22 inches as compared to 7.8 inches in Albuquerque, and it can be 20 degrees cooler at the Crest than in the city. Wind, another factor determining plant life, creates an even greater differential. Along the Crest, where the primary southwest winds often whip against the mountain, the vegetation is much sparser than in the same Hudsonian zone just below the ridge line on the east side. The east side in general is denser than the exposed, wind-buffeted western face of the mountains.

Descending through the life zones, higher temperatures and less rainfall determine the nature of plant growth. Ponderosa pine is much less dense than spruce and fir, and different species of bush and wildflower better suited for hot weather replace their higher-elevation relatives. Often the same wildflower has a low-country and a high-country variety, the former being smaller and more clumped, and perhaps a different color; the western wall flower is an example.

Animal life in the Sandias also varies from zone to zone. Fifty-eight species of mammal, 225 bird species, 34 reptile species, and six amphibian species all live in one zone or another with seasonal and conditional crossovers. In each trail description, I mention the animals one may see along the way. There are many more that one will probably never see, but they too are part of the Sandias.

Probably the Sandias' best-known creature is the Rocky Mountain bighorn sheep. Introduced to the mountains in the 1940s, the sheep seemed to do well for a while, their number increasing from six to nearly 300. By 1978, when I patrolled the Crest Trail for the Forest Service, that number had dwindled dramatically, although I still often saw the bighorns, underneath the Tramway towers or descending the rock face below Kiwanis Meadow. A survey conducted by the New Mexico Game and Fish Department in 1982 counted only six sheep.

What happened to the bighorns is still speculative, but three factors contributed to their demise: internal parasites, poaching, and habitat pressures due to increased human use of the mountains. The Manzano bighorn herd seems to be faring a little better. In 1977 and 1978, 16 sheep from the Pecos Wilderness were released in the Manzanos; in 1982, 35 were counted.

Other animal populations, including the black bear and the mountain lion, are also experiencing the impact of habitat intrusion. A group of bears, estimated to be about 12 in number, lives on the east side of the Sandias. According the the Game and Fish Department, five mountain lions have been sighted recently. Again, the Manzano populations are larger: approximately 50 bears and 35 mountain lions roam the wilderness.

Many animal species proliferate, however: mule deer, foxes, rabbits, squirrels, chipmunks, coyotes, snakes, and birds. Two hundred and twenty-five species of birds have been sighted, including the golden and bald eagles and the peregrine falcon, an endangered species. Golden eagles have nested in the cliffs above the Cañon de Domingo Baca for years, although several males have been shot. A pair of peregrines has nested in the Sandias for the past several years, and an official closure is in effect at the nesting site, prohibiting rock climbers from using the area from June 21 to August 15. The summer of 1982 was a success—three peregrine fledglings were hatched and reared.

Trails

In this guide, trails are presented as systems rather than by individual descriptions. This is to provide hikers with the information to plan more than round-trip hikes going out and back on the same trail. Seeing new country along an entire hike is usually more appealing than backtracking, and it enables the hiker to learn more of the mountains on each day's outing. Most of the individual trails will be included in these systems; the few that are not will be listed separately. Transportation to and from trailheads can present problems, of course, if you leave a car at the beginning of one trail and emerge from another, so I have provided some hints about leaving cars at the various trailheads.

All of the described systems can be hiked in a day (except those in the Manzanos so listed). Unlike some of the larger wilderness areas, both the Sandias and the Manzanos lend themselves to day trips, and I want to emphasize the accessibility of the wilderness experience to everyone, not just backpackers. Any of these trips could be turned into an overnight adventure, or joined with others for an excursion of several days. Backpacking is allowed in both districts, contrary to the confused belief that it is prohibited in the Sandias (it is prohibited *only* in the picnic areas).

The trails are listed in the ascending order of difficulty, or as close as I can come to this in a subjective ordering. Degree of difficulty is usually defined by terrain, elevation ascent and descent, and mileage. I have used my experience with each trail to evaluate all these criteria and to make my own categorization. Many hikers will find that they disagree with me, but I think the order presented here will help the beginner to choose routes wisely. I list an approximate hiking time at the end of each chapter, but remember, this is only a rough estimate, based on a moderate pace with time out for lunch, looking at views, or examining wildflowers. Some hikers will complete the hikes in less time; others will stretch a walk into a full, leisurely day.

Preparation for Hiking

I always carry a day pack with me when heading out for a hike, be it one mile or ten. In it are at least one quart of water (two, if it's summer), a jacket, something to eat, matches, a map, and sunscreen. Each of these items indicates areas of concern that all hikers should consider and plan for.

Maps

I personally love maps. I like being able to stand on a ridge, look at the map, and pinpoint where I am in the scheme of things. It's best not to be fanatical about it, though, and become so dependent on the map that you forget it's only an aid to outdoor enjoyment, and not the focal point. Knowing how to read a map is like knowing the names of wildflowers and birds—knowledge facilitates a larger understanding and better appreciation of detail.

Accompanying each trail description is a map showing the general area of the hike, the trailhead, and the route followed. Many kinds of maps detailing various aspects of the Manzanos and Sandias are available. The Forest Service is the place to go for a general map of the two ranger districts, including forest boundaries, roads, trails, and developed picnic areas. This Cibola National Forest map is sold at the Sandia Ranger Station in Tijeras, the Mountainair Ranger Station in Mountainair, or the Cibola National Forest Supervisor's Office in Albuquerque. Also available through the Forest Service is a map of the two wilderness areas.

Topography maps by the U.S. Geological Survey break the Sandias and Manzanos down into quadrants and detail the elevations. These maps are good for exploring new places or for climbing off the trails into canyons or along ridges. They can show you what to expect in terms of difficulty of terrain. These are available at several stores in town or from the U.S. Geological Survey Denver distribution office.

Clothing

Choice of clothing is largely personal, of course, but two particular areas need to be discussed: footwear and garments for bad weather.

If you don't wear suitable, comfortable hiking shoes you won't enjoy your hike. Feet are the number one consideration. I almost always wear hiking boots with Vibram soles, but I don't think that has to be a hard-and-fast rule. Modern-day running shoes or sneakers with their specially-designed soles for jogging work well for hiking. If a trail is relatively free of rocks and gullies and loose gravel, and if the weather is temperate, running shoes are perfectly adequate.

High-topped leather hiking boots with Vibram soles provide the best support for your feet and the best protection against injury. They are essential in inclement weather and rough terrain.

On the loose gravel of the Piedra Liza Trail, for example, even the best running shoe is useless. Walking over rocks and roots and depressions can quickly wear out a pair of feet in sneakers, and the possibility of injury is less with the stronger support of a boot—fewer twisted ankles, bruised heels and toes, and blisters. Be sure to break in new boots before attempting a five-mile hike, though, or they won't prevent blisters either. Heavy socks should cushion the feet in boots. A heavy cotton sock is adequate in summer; in the winter, try a light cotton sock under a wool one.

Because mountain weather can change dramatically in a relatively short time, I always carry some sort of jacket in my pack. In the dry, exceedingly hot days of June I prepare for the unexpected but entirely possible afternoon thundershower with a rain poncho. In the wetter months of July and August I also carry a sweatshirt jacket for wear under the poncho in case of steady drizzle. In the fall I dispense with poncho and add gloves and a hat to the jacket; despite a warm day in town, a mountain chill can almost always be felt.

Whether one wears shorts and a halter top or long pants and a cotton shirt for summer hiking is mostly personal, but consider a few factors. The summer sun is very intense; if your skin is sensitive, choose the latter outfit. The higher the elevation, the less atmosphere there is to filter the sun's rays, so beware. I always use sunscreen on my face, or wear a brimmed hat. Take the terrain into account also when deciding what to wear; if the trail is not maintained and leads through dense vegetation, wear enough clothing to prevent scrapes and cuts from bushes and branches.

Water

There are numerous springs in the Sandias and the Manzanos, both in the high country and at the lower elevations. Some are denoted on the maps by the symbol, ⚡ , but there are many more to be found by exploring the canyons and arroyos. It is wise never to depend upon them as a source of drinking water, however, for two reasons: (1) some of them periodically dry up, and (2) the Forest Service recommends that one never drink from mountain springs because of possible bacterial contamination.

Familiarity with the springs in all seasons helps one know which are the most dependable water sources, but I always carry at least one quart of water from home. In the summer I carry two quarts of water or herbal tea, freezing them the night before so that the ice melts slowly on the hike, providing a nice, cool drink.

During the spring runoff and the July-August rainy season many canyons and arroyos carry small streams down the mountain. This is the water one must be most careful about, as there is more chance of contamination the further the water is from its underground source, the spring. Also, water flowing near heavy population centers, such as picnic grounds, is more likely to be contaminated than that found in more isolated areas.

There are several ways to treat the mountain water if it is necessary to use it. Iodine or halazone pills can be purchased, or campers may want to boil water before use. For hikers it's just common sense to carry their own water; campers, who need more water, should weigh the information.

Emergencies

Many agencies and authorities say that you should never hike alone. I can understand that advice, but I cannot say that I always abide by it. It limits your sense of freedom and stands between you and experiences that you may want to have on your own. If I do decide to hike alone, though, I adhere to a cardinal rule: I always tell someone where I am hiking and when I expect to return. Then, if I don't show up within a reasonable period of time, the proper authorities can be notified.

All missing hikers should be reported to the New Mexico State Police. They will coordinate the search, utilizing highly-skilled search and rescue teams, the Forest Service, the county sheriff's department, and whomever else they need.

If you decide to hike alone it's a good idea to carry an emergency first aid kit. Small cuts, bruises, and abrasions can be treated on the trail to help prevent infection until further treatment is available. Hikers often ask me if a snakebite kit should be included in the first aid equipment. My advice is no; according to the American Red Cross, an incision made to suction the venom should only be administered as a last resort, when there is no medical help nearby and the victim is suffering respiration problems.

Hikers should be aware of rattlesnakes, however, and of alternative treatments for snakebite. Contrary to popular belief, rattlesnakes are found above the desert-foothills zone of the Sandias and the Manzanos. I once saw one at the top of Embudito Trail, a 9,000-foot elevation. But don't ruin your hiking with snake paranoia. The rattlers I've seen have always seen me first and noisily warned me of their presence. Their rattle is a defensive gesture, and like most animals, a rattler will not attack unless provoked.

If you *do* get bitten by a rattlesnake, try not to panic. A snake's venom is carried through the system in the bloodstream, and if one's adrenalin is flowing, the blood will be pumped that much faster. Stay as calm as possible, and immobilize the area of the bite. If you are hiking with a friend, send him or her for medical help and stay put, preferably lying down. If you are hiking by yourself, decide what to do according to your circumstances. If you are on a heavily-traveled trail, lie down and wait for someone to come along and then send them for help. If it is unlikely that anyone will come by or if you are only a short distance from a trailhead, walk out on the trail to the nearest phone or medical facility. You can also apply a "restrictive" band (*not* a tourniquet) two to four inches above the bite to help restrict the blood flow. Watch for swelling, and loosen the band if necessary.

Only if medical help is four or five hours away and severe symptoms occur (impaired breathing, unconsciousness) should an incision over the wound be made and the venom suctioned A high risk of infection classifies this as a last-resort treatment.

A footnote about getting lost. With this book in your pocket, you won't *ever* get lost, of course, but if for some strange reason you do, remember these few things: (1) If you are not hurt and have the energy to find your way out, walk downhill and you will eventually re-enter civilization. (2) If you *are* hurt or too tired to negotiate any more walking, sit down and wait for someone to find you. If you have notified someone at home about where you planned to hike, the search and rescue team will find you fast. If you didn't tell anyone where you planned to hike, they will still find you, but it might take a while. Don't panic, stay put, and make a shelter against the weather.

Hypothermia

Hypothermia is the chilling of the inner core of the human body, with the body losing heat faster than it can produce it. This is caused by exposure to cold and is aggravated by overtiring, wet clothing, and wind chill. Although a well-prepared hiker should not worry too much about this, hypothermia is dangerous enough so that everyone should know its symptoms and, more important, how to prevent it.

The symptoms include shivering, slurred and incoherent

speech, stumbling, drowsiness, exhaustion. It may result in death. Prevention is all-important. Understand what hypothermia is and know what environmental factors lead to exposure: wet clothes, wind, over-exertion (reaching the top of the mountain or else), loss of fluids. Know what to do if any of these conditions occur. Get out of rainy, windy weather as quickly as possible, eat and drink enough to support your physical activity, don't be afraid to stop and rest or to turn back. If hypothermia is detected, drastic treatment is in order: get the victim to shelter, remove all wet clothing, administer warm drinks, get him or her into dry clothing and a sleeping bag. If the victim is semi-conscious, skin-to-skin contact is the best treatment. Strip the victim's clothes off and put him or her into a sleeping bag with another person. Transport the victim to a hospital if possible, or go for help.

Fire Restrictions

During critical parts of the summer both the Sandias and the Manzanos may be put under fire restrictions because of dry weather and potential fire hazard. Restrictions can prohibit smoking and campfires or mandate a total closure of the forest. Check with the local ranger district to see what, if any, restrictions are in effect. For fire prevention and environmental reasons, the Forest Service is currently requesting that hikers and campers refrain from building campfires altogether. Instead, a gas backpacking stove for cooking is recommended.

Trail Maintenance

The following is a list of trail maintenance volunteer groups for the Sandia Mountains:

Embudito: Sierra Club
10K-Osha Loop: Sandia Wildlife Club
Faulty: Girl Scouts
Cienega: University of New Mexico ROTC
North Crest: Boy Scouts, Troop #189
South Crest: New Mexico Mountain Club
Tramway: Central New Mexico Audubon Society
Three Gun: YWCA
Survey: New Mexico Ski Touring Club
Piedra Liza: Albuquerque Wildlife Federation
Cienega Nature Trail: Sandia Mountain Lions Club
Cañoncito: Boy Scouts, Troop #185

Tree Spring, Upper Faulty, Crest Spur: Boy Scouts,
    Troop #496
La Luz: University of New Mexico Mountain Club
La Cueva: Breakfast Exchange Club

PART II.
HIKING TRAILS IN THE SANDIA MOUNTAINS

NORTH CREST—10K

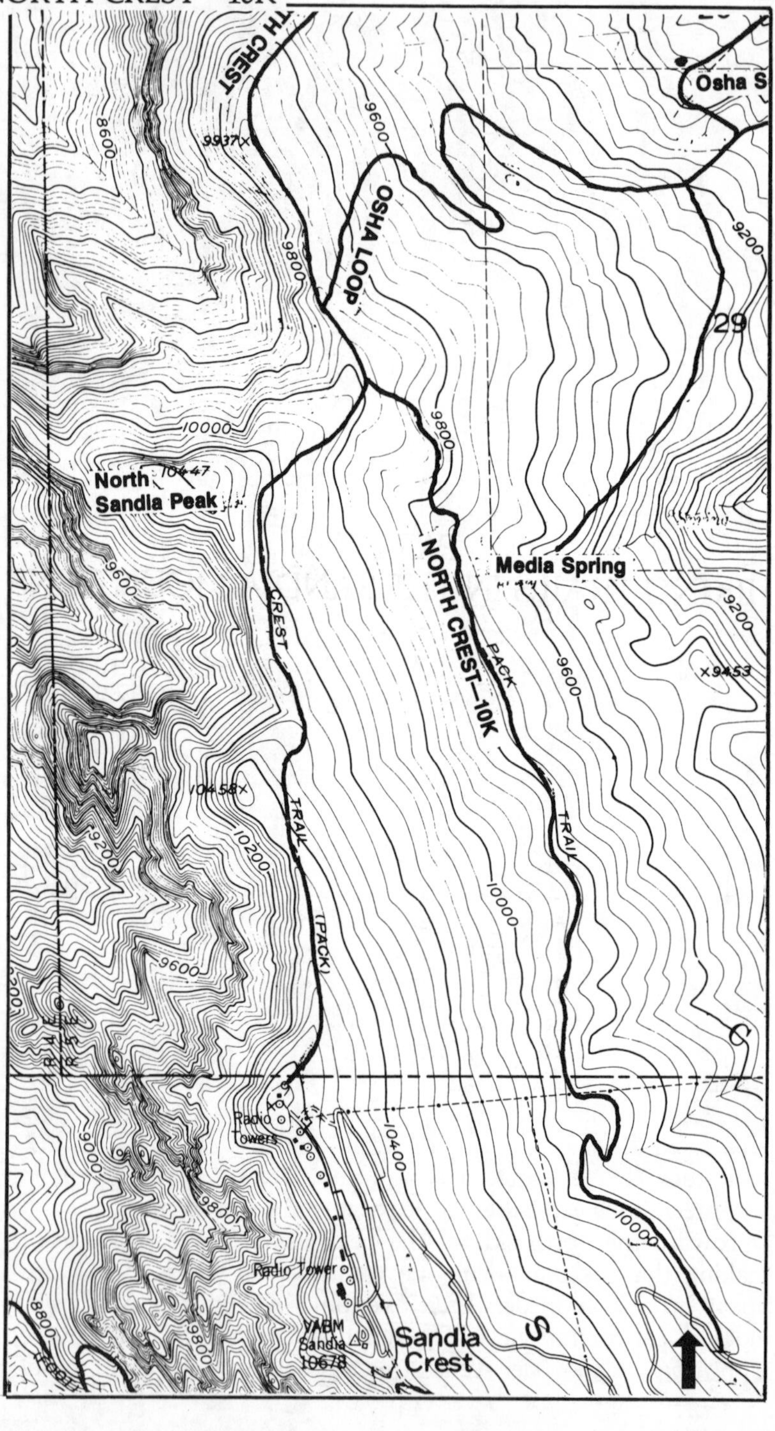

NORTH CREST (#130)—10K (CANON MEDIA) *4.5 miles*

North Crest Trail begins at Sandia Crest parking lot and continues north 11 miles to Tunnel Spring near Placitas. Instead of following the entire trail to Tunnel Spring, this hike makes a loop back to the Crest Highway (State Road 536) for a shorter, more diverse trip.

Transportation for this hike is relatively easy. The trailhead is just north of the Crest parking lot on Crest Highway, and the end of the hike is on the same road two miles below the Crest. As you drive towards the Crest, near the top are several cleared areas on your right (north) where there is room to pull off the road and park. The first of the roadcuts that traverse the side of the mountain is where the 10K Trail emerges (3.7 miles from the junction of State Road 44 and the Crest Highway). There is no sign here, but the trail is marked with blue, diamond-shaped cross-country ski blazes, visible from the road. 10K Trail, named for the fact that it begins and ends at a 10,000-foot elevation (K=1,000), continues south across the Crest Highway, traverses the ski area, and emerges at the junction of Tree Spring and South Crest Trails. Leave a car at the pull-off and continue to the Crest parking lot.

North Crest Trail follows the line of the Crest for the first two miles. Just north of the television and radio towers, there are several spectacular overlooks (little spur trails lead out to them) above Chimney Canyon. You can see many of the rock formations also visible from Albuquerque, including the Needle, the Prow, and the Shield; the latter is actually the face of North Peak. The trail continues back into the woods as it passes North Peak toward the Cañon del Agua overlook.

The upper part of the trail really feels like the forest primeval: huge spruce and fir shadow the path and provide a cool, moist climate where mushrooms and orchids grow. I have seen the fairy slipper orchid here, alongside larkspur, Solomon plume, geranium and penstemon. At North Peak an unmaintained trail leads out to the top of the peak and down to the edge of the Shield, where one can actually walk across the top of this huge rock face. It's a dangerous trail, due to a lot of scrambling and precipitous exposures, so leave it to the adventurer.

Toward the north side of the peak aspen grow in profusion, making this hike an ideal one for the fall. Suddenly the trail opens up at Cañon del Agua overlook, where a rock wall provides a seat for the view. The north side of the peak is covered with aspen; Cañon del Agua stretches below to the Rio Grande.

Both Mount Taylor and the Jemez Mountains are visible from here (by the way, that's the town of Bernalillo you're seeing down by the river).

North Crest Trail continues through the oak as it heads down the northeast side of the mountains. The junction with 10K Trail lies just where Crest Trail emerges from the aspen into the opening at the overlook. There is no trail marker, but the trees are blazed with blue cross-country diamonds. 10K drops down the east side of the mountains toward the spring at the head of Cañon Media. A short walk through the forest leads to the uppermost roadcut traversing the mountain. This one crosses all the way to the ridge of the mountains where it intersects North Crest Trail at what is called the north Cañon del Agua overlook, marked by another stone bench.

These roadcuts are the result of bureaucratic bungling. In the 1960s the Forest Service bowed to various pressures and decided to re-route the Crest Highway to make a scenic "skyline" drive traversing the ridgeline of the Sandias to Placitas. Work was already begun—hence the series of roadcuts—before enough people heard about the plan and objected to the impact such a road would have on the forest environment. By this time it was the early 1970s and the nation was in the midst of the so-called energy crisis. The government's de-emphasis on automobile use helped to halt the project. The roadcuts have started to fill in with new growth and make good cross-country ski trails, but they remain a testimony of poor planning and insensitivity.

The trail crosses the roadcut and heads back into the trees. A half mile later, a sign on a tree marks the turnoff down to Media Spring. Unfortunately, someone, in mistaken helpfulness, inscribed "Osha Spring" on the sign. Osha Spring is in the next canyon to the north, Cañon Osha; some of the old maps have Cañons Osha and Media transposed, and apparently the sign maker used the wrong map.

The short but steep climb down to the spring is worth a side trip. A beautiful meadow appears where a box spring catches the cold, clear water—it's the perfect stopping place to lie in the grass, eat lunch, and even fall asleep. The bears of the Sandias also frequent Cañon Media; their claw marks, high up on the aspens, are the evidence. In the fall, rose-breasted nuthatches congregate in the meadow before their migration south.

After lunch, climb back to the trail and continue south, traversing the heads of Cañon Media and Las Huertas Canyon back to the Crest Highway. The terrain is up and down, a relatively easy two-mile hike if slowly paced. At several places the forest opens up for views down into Las Huertas Canyon, but for the most part one hikes under a canopy of spruce, fir, and aspen. I have seen the fairy slipper orchid along this trail too, amidst a myriad of high-country wildflowers. Toward the end of the trail are several junctions where paths to the right are blazed with blue diamonds. Don't worry, these are only alternative routes for cross-country skiers to avoid steep places and they re-enter the main trail in a few-hundred yards. The trail emerges just above the roadcut where the car is parked, and it's only a short trip back to the Crest to retrieve the other car.

Approximate hiking time is four hours.

SOUTH CREST (#130)—10K *5 miles*

This hike begins along the well-worn Crest Trail between Sandia Crest and the Tramway and continues along South Crest Trail to the junction of 10K where it loops back to the Crest Highway (State Road 536). It's an easy five-mile hike, downhill most of the way.

Leave a car at the pull-off on the Crest Highway where the northern part of 10K Trail emerges, as described on page 19. The southern part of 10K Trail, included in this hike, continues on the south side of the Crest Highway, 0.2 miles below the pull-off. Continue from the pull-off up to the Crest parking lot where the hike begins.

You've probably been on this first 1.5-mile stretch before, since it's the most accessible in the Sandia trail system. It begins at the bottom of the stairs, where the Crest Spur, connecting with the La Luz Trail, goes off to the right. You can follow the Crest Trail left or right at the beginning of the nature loop, a few feet down the path. This is a short, guided tour of the plant life in this uppermost life zone (signs on barrier posts) and a nice introduction to the Crest area. The Crest Trail continues on from the loop toward Kiwanis Meadow.

Most people walk out along the ridge to Kiwanis Cabin for a look at the spectacular scenery in the Cañon de Domingo Baca and in the upper Cañon la Cueva where the La Luz Trail comes up. The Crest Trail actually dips through the trees before the cabin and crosses the southwest corner of Kiwanis Meadow following the ridgeline east. It then re-enters the trees to the south toward the Tram. From here it's almost all downhill, in and out of the trees, until you come to another loop trail which leads a guided nature tour along the ridgeline above the Tram. The Crest Trail emerges onto a path lined with low rock walls just on the north side of the restaurant.

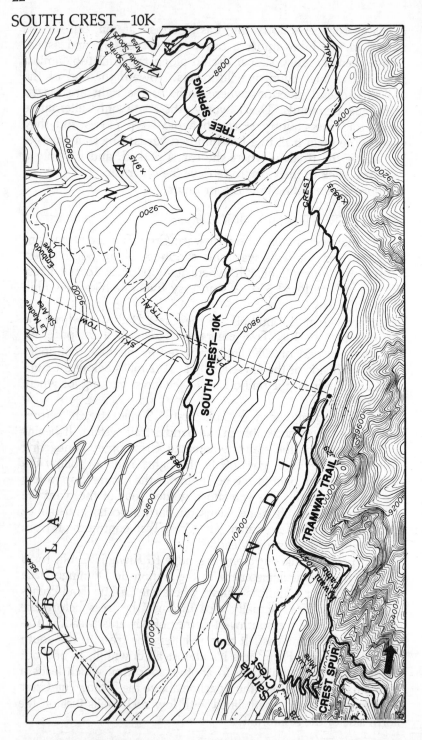

After eating, drinking, and looking at people, views, and the Forest Service Visitor's Center, you will find the continuation of the Crest Trail on the south side of the Tram, down by the water treatment plant. There may or may not be a sign there, but the trail is obvious. It follows the ridgeline south, just on the east side, down through the spruce and fir of the high country. There's a rock ledge lookout above Cañon de Domingo Baca, looking south to Pino and Bear Canyons. Here the trail switchbacks to the northeast for quite a distance, before turning south again. I've seen the unusual monkshood here, along with figwort, lousewort, columbine, and golden draba.

The trail heads into oak near the 10K junction, where views to the east open up. A spur trail to the west heads up to the rock ledge and overlook above Pino Canyon. The Tram towers can be seen to the north, along with the Kiwanis Meadow ridge. This is a good place for lunch, if there aren't too many people sharing the popular overlook and possibly spoiling your reverie.

Continue south on the Crest Trail to where it loops around to the northeast and the junction of three trails: 10K Trail heading north, Tree Spring Trail heading downhill to State Road 44, and the continuation of South Crest Trail all the way to Tijeras Canyon. We turn north on 10K Trail and make an easy two-mile hike across the ski area to the Crest Highway. The trail stays in oak until Cañon Madera, where it enters the forest primeval, innumerable wildflowers lining the path. It's a down-and-up hike across the canyon—the uphill is the only steep part of this hike— to the first of the ski slopes running down the mountain. Cross-country ski blazes mark the entry and emergence of each of the eight slopes you cross. Sometimes you have to look closely to find them, but as the trail basically traverses the mountain the blazes are evident without too much looking up and down for them. The slopes are covered with lush grass and lots of golden pea; it's fun to converse with the folks on the chairlift as they pass overhead.

Columbine, osha, geranium, and violets line the fairly level three-quarter mile hike up to the Highway. As you come to an old jeep trail leading up from the Crest Highway, there is a wooden sign on a fir tree marking the trail. Cross-country ski blazes mark the rest of the way out along the jeep trail to the Crest Highway. (Since the wooden marker is not visible from the road, the best way to find this half of 10K Trail if you're going south is to park at the pull-off up the road and walk down the highway .2 miles until you see the blue blazes marking the jeep trail.)

Approximate hiking time is four hours.

TREE SPRING—SOUTH CREST—CIENEGA

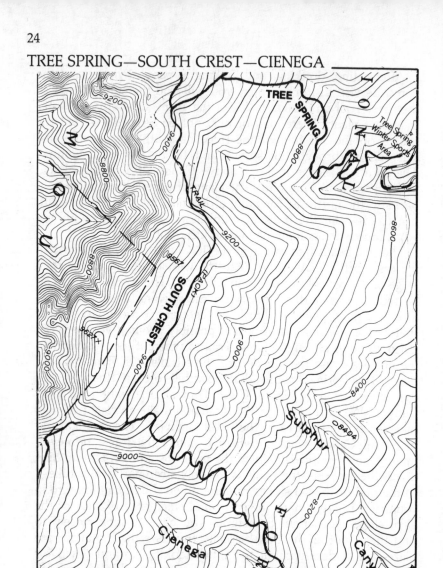

TREE SPRING (#147)—SOUTH CREST (#130)—
CIENEGA (#148) *6 miles*

The ascent up Tree Spring Trail to South Crest Trail is the most gradual of the uphill climbs, beginning at 8,500 feet and ending two miles later at 9,500 feet.

The trailhead is on the east side of the mountains on State Road 44, about one mile south of the Sandia Peak Ski Area. Take I-40 east to the Sandia Crest–North 14 exit, and continue on North 14 for eight miles to the junction with SR 44. Turn west on SR 44 to Sandia Crest and proceed 5.7 miles to the Tree Spring trailhead. There is parking space available on the downhill side of SR 44; a small wooden marker designates the trail (there's an outhouse there too). Tree Spring Trail is named for the spring south of the trailhead alongside the highway.

The trail is wide and well-worn through the ponderosa pine in the Transition zone, heavily wooded for the first mile or so. Wildflowers are abundant: wild iris, wild rose, clematis, mariposa lily, osha, western wall flower, wild parsley. This is one of the trails where you might see a mule deer.

As you approach the spruce-fir climatic zone the woods occasionally open up for magnificent views of the San Pedro Mountains to the east. The Sangre de Cristo Mountains above Santa Fe can be seen to the northeast. The last half-mile of the trail climbs into aspen and Gambel oak, and the views are momentarily lost.

Just below the ridgeline Tree Spring Trail intersects two trails, South Crest and 10K. To the north along South Crest Trail lies Sandia Peak Tramway, a steep 1.5-mile climb. To the south lies our route, 1.75 miles to the junction with Cienega Trail.

10K Trail, one of the newest in the Forest Service trail system, is described on page 19. This trail heads north from Tree Spring and traverses the east side of the mountain, through Sandia Peak Ski Area, over to the Crest Highway, and on across the mountain to the Cañon del Agua overlook on North Crest Trail.

Before heading out toward Cienega you should take the short path that leads up to the ridgeline of the Sandias. Follow South Crest Trail north instead of south, as if you were headed to the Tram, then turn west on an obvious path that climbs the last few feet to the incredible view from the top of the mountains. Standing over Pino Canyon one can see Albuquerque spread out below, a sprawling eruption of miniature houses speckled with green. The horizon is defined by Mount Taylor to the west, Ladron Peak and the Magdalena Mountains to the south, and the steep ridgeline of Cañon de Domingo Baca where the Tram ascends the mountains to the north.

When your feelings of awe have somewhat abated, go back to the Tree Spring–Crest Trail junction and continue south. South Crest Trail follows the ridgeline of the Sandias just on the east side. It's a fairly level hike except for two rather steep inclines near the end of the 1.75-mile hike to the Cienega Trail. The Crest Trail is lined with Gambel oak; osha, mint, geraniums, and sweet cicely proliferate. I usually stop for lunch after the last incline of the trail, preferring downhill action after eating. Sitting beneath one of the big firs on the west side of the trail I can see I-40 stretching away to Tucumcari and, on a clear day, the Gallinas Mountains rising to the southeast. Near this picnic spot, if you look closely, wild onions can be found growing amongst the mountain grasses under the trees.

The rest of the trail is downhill to the junction with Cienega Trail. Another westward view is available a few steps up on the rocks above the junction, looking down over Bear Canyon. Turn east on Cienega Trail, and it's 2.25 miles down the trail to Cienega Picnic Ground. The trail is considerably steeper than Tree Spring Trail and for those with weak knees not a good way to descend. The upper half of the trail is very rocky, and I recommend hiking boots rather than running shoes or sneakers for protection and support. The trail is badly eroded in places, basically following the gullies down the mountain. (The last time I hiked Cienega the volunteer group maintaining the trail had done a lot of work to re-route the path around the gullies.)

You stay in thick forest all the way down, so attention to details takes the place of looking at views. Wild strawberries line the path; in mid- to late summer one can taste the small, very sweet berries. Toward the end of the trail the terrain levels out considerably. You are apt to meet other hikers here, folks from Cienega Picnic Ground who have ventured out on the easy part of the trail. Depending on the time of year and how much snow has fed the water table, Cienega Spring trickles or rushes alongside the trail about one-quarter of a mile above the picnic ground. Both spring and hiker emerge from the woods just above the Cienega parking lot; the hike is over.

The directions to Cienega Picnic Ground are the same as to Tree Spring, only the distance is shorter. After you turn off North 14 to SR 44, drive through the entry to Cibola National Forest. Cienega Picnic Ground is the first turn to the left beyond the forest boundary. Follow the entry road up the hill (a road off to the right leads to Sulphur Picnic Ground) to the stop sign; then turn right and continue past the entrance to the Nature Trail for the Handicapped until the road enters the parking lot. Leave one car here and drive the second car back out to SR 44 and on up the highway to Tree Spring trailhead.

Approximate leisurely hiking time is four hours.

CANONCITO (#150)—FAULTY (#195)—
SOUTH CREST (#130) 6.75 miles

This hike begins on Cañoncito Trail and traverses the east side of the Sandias until it connects with the lower portion of South Crest Trail. It is one of the most evenly paced hikes on the mountain, staying at about a 7,500-foot elevation for the entire route.

To find the Cañoncito trailhead, take I-40 east to the Sandia Crest–North 14 turnoff. Continue on North 14 about 3.5 miles to the town of Cañoncito. A sign on the right-hand side of the road indicates the turn onto Forest Road 299 which leads to Cañoncito and Cole Spring Picnic Ground. Turn left onto FR 299 and follow the road past the turn to the town of Cañon-cito and into the canyon. At 1.7 miles a sign marks the trailhead; there is room to park alongside the road.

The climb up to Cañoncito Spring and the junction with Faulty Trail is an easy three-fourths mile hike. The trail passes through piñon-juniper, with some amazingly large alligator junipers along the way. When you hear the bubbling of the spring be sure to follow the trail carefully and don't head straight up the canyon. Look for watercress growing in some of the pools along the trail.

At Cañoncito Spring the trail enters an open area where people often camp. Continue through the opening, following the spring; the junction with Faulty Trail is at the place where the spring emerges from the ground. The trail sign gives the length to South Crest Trail as five miles.

Cañoncito Trail continues up the canyon until it intersects South Crest Trail high up on the ridgeline of the mountains. Faulty Trail turns south to traverse the east side. This trail has a mysterious history. Blazes on the trees in the shape of diamonds mark the route, and the trail was originally called the Diamond Trail. The Forest Service keeps it secret who originally cleared the trail, but rumor has it that a group of local people regularly rode their horses along the route for years before anyone else discovered it. The trail was officially incorporated into the trail system in 1981. In 1984 Faulty was also blazed north from

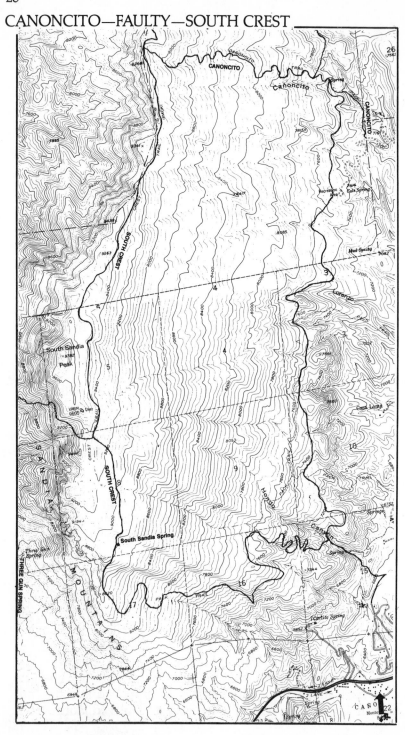

Cañoncito to the junction with Cienega Trail.

The trail stays mostly in the Transition zone of ponderosa pine, with occasional breaks in the tree line for views to the east. At about 0.7 miles there is a path leading a quarter of a mile down into the Cole Spring Picnic Ground, the Forest Service picnic area at the end of Cañoncito Road.

The reason for re-naming the trail from Diamond to Faulty becomes obvious a couple of miles into the hike. Rows of rock, looking like man-made walls, descend the mountain across the trail. These are "dikes," fissures filled with igneous rock moved up from a lower fracture, or "fault." Hence the name, Faulty Trail.

On the second half of the trail the views start to look toward the southeast; you can see the microwave tower and fire lookout on Cedro Peak in the Manzanitas. Several meadows provide good lunch spots. In the meadow just to the west of the trail is where the Upper Faulty Trail begins. This spur trail also traverses the east side, almost parallel to the main trail, and connects with South Crest Trail a mile farther north of the main Faulty junction.

A steep decline at the end of the trail leads to the junction with South Crest Trail. To the right the Crest Trail continues up toward South Peak; to the left, the trail is only one mile to Canyon Estates, South Crest trailhead.

As you head down the canyon to the trailhead some deciduous trees appear, denoting a spring. The trail crosses the trickling water as it flows down over a travertine formation—limestone deposits from hot spring water flowing down the mountain. At the turn of the next switchback an old trail descends to the east towards the little town of Hobbes (actually, the few houses where the Hobbes family lived). At the next switchback a spur trail crosses over the spring and leads up to a shallow cave in the rocks. This is a good place to take a break before the last little leg of the trip to Canyon Estates.

To reach South Crest trailhead by car, take I-40 east to the Tijeras–South 14 turnoff. Turn left at the stop sign (right takes you to Tijeras), go under the overpass, and follow the road right into Canyon Estates. The road continues through the housing development to the parking lot at the trailhead. The best way to arrange transportation for this hike is to take two cars. Drive to the South Crest trailhead and leave one car there. Continue in the other car back out of Canyon Estates under the freeway to the turn to North 14. This road connects with the North 14 freeway exit, so follow the instructions given at the

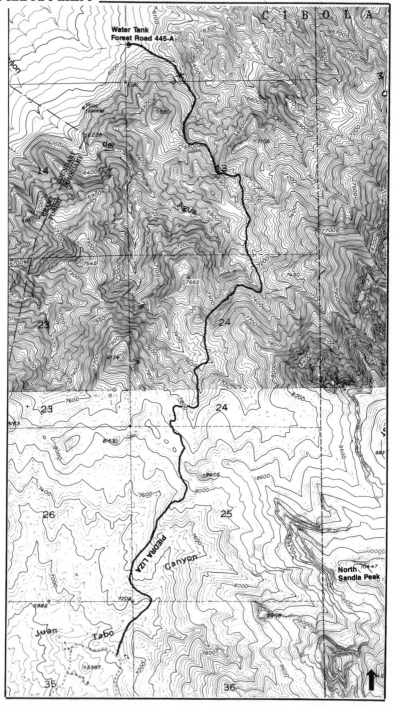

beginning of this section for getting to the Cañoncito trailhead. A trip back at the end of the hike retrieves the second car. A word of warning about the road into Cañoncito: when it rains heavily, the road is almost impassable because of the mud. Save this hike for a sunny day.

Approximate hiking time is four to five hours.

PIEDRA LIZA (#135) *5 miles*

This low-country hike begins in Juan Tabo Canyon, climbs Juan Tabo Ridge (the Rincón), and descends Cañon del Agua to the Bernalillo watershed. The trail never ascends more than about 8,000 feet, so I recommend it as a fall hike, when the weather is a little cooler. Or wear a hat and lots of sunscreen.

The trailhead is about one mile beyond Juan Tabo Picnic Ground on Forest Road 333D. Take Tramway Boulevard north past the turnoff to the Tramway; then take the first turn to the right after the riding stables onto Forest Road 333 (there may or may not be a sign). Follow the blacktop up the canyon past La Cueva Picnic Ground, Juan Tabo Picnic Ground, and the turnoff to the La Luz Trail. The pavement ends and the road becomes dirt as it turns to the right. Follow the dirt road back through the houses; Piedra Liza trailhead is on the right, and there is a parking area to the left.

Piedra Liza is classified as a primitive trail, which it is as far as trail conditions go. One must pay close attention to the trail so as not to lose it, and I recommend hiking boots for the steep, washed-out sections of the descent.

The trail starts climbing immediately and then briefly levels out as it enters Waterfall Canyon. Normally a spring flows across the trail here, down from the waterfall that names this small subsidiary canyon in Juan Tabo Canyon. Two forks of the canyon converge here, and in the saddle between them you can follow a primitive trail a little over a mile up to the base of the Prow, a favorite climbing formation. This is called the Movie Trail, since it was made for the motion picture *Lonely Are the Brave*, which was partially filmed here. There is a trail to the waterfall which begins here also, a 0.9-mile hike up Waterfall Canyon; every time I have made this rough climb, the water has been flowing.

Piedra Liza begins climbing out of Waterfall Canyon immediately in the direction of Juan Tabo Ridge. This is piñon-juniper country, hot and dry. The cacti love it: yucca, hedgehog, cholla, and prickly pear are abundant. Owls seem fond of it too; I've flushed more owls off piñon trees here than any other place in the mountains. In the fall, this is the place to come to pick piñon nuts, if there are any. The crop comes in cycles; in some years the trail will be covered with nuts, in others there's not a one to be found.

From the trail you can see up the rugged west face of Juan Tabo Canyon to the television and radio towers on the Crest. The Needle, the Shield, and the Prow are clearly visible all along the 1.5-mile climb to the ridge. You can also see the dead trees from the old Chimney Canyon fire, just below the TV towers. These smaller canyons of Juan Tabo Canyon are the most rugged on the mountain, and are not recommended for bushwhacking your way to the top. About three-quarters of the way up, the switchbacks begin and the ridgeline appears imminent, although the climb seems interminable. A narrow saddle marks the end of the climb. Juan Tabo Canyon has been left behind; Cañon del Agua looms to the north.

This is a good place to rest, and a great place to take a look at the view. A short trail just to the east of the saddle leads up to a lookout on an outcrop of rocks above Juan Tabo Canyon. To the east is the rock face of the Sandias; the view sweeps around to the west to include Albuquerque, Mount Taylor, the Jemez and the Sangre de Cristos. You can see all of Cañon del Agua ahead where Piedra Liza descends to the north side of the mountains.

Back in the saddle the trail quickly starts down into the south fork of Cañon del Agua. Huge ponderosa pines supplement the piñon-juniper vegetation. Stop and smell the ponderosa bark; a sweet smell of vanilla invades your senses. In the fall, you can see a yellow swath of aspens covering the back side of the Shield.

The trail emerges into the sandy bottom of an arroyo and follows the arroyo north. Look closely, and about 50 yards along the arroyo a clearing opens up to the right. Tall ponderosas circle rock-lined fire pits that campers have made. In a wet year a spring runs down the canyon just to the north of this clearing. It's a good place to eat lunch—the trip is half over. This lunch spot is actually on private land, an old homesteading section in the middle of the forest. Back on the trail, past the half-way marker, you pass the old stone foundation of a cabin. Originally a mining claim, the private land had access from a wagon road leading up from Piedra Liza Spring in the Bernalillo watershed.

Now begins the last short climb to the saddle between the north and south forks of Cañon del Agua. It's a bit hard to take on a full stomach, but it's over soon. The rest is all downhill. The trail winds its way down Cañon del Agua into piñon-juniper country again. Several springs cross the path, providing welcome relief. Now is when hiking boots become imperative. Although various Forest Service groups and volunteers have worked on the trail over the years, it remains sketchy, rocky, and steep. Lots of loose gravel compounds the problem. Take it slow, watch the trail and your footing, and you'll do fine. The canyon you are in is narrow, and even if you momentarily lose the trail, you'll soon figure out where you should be. The only way to go is down.

For most of the hike you can see the Rio Grande, Bernalillo, and State Road 44 to Placitas. Just before the trail emerges at an old watering tank, a side canyon leads up to Piedra Liza Spring. It's a boxed spring for wildlife and a good place to bird watch. Some of the water from the spring flows down the canyon to the trailhead over the flat, white rocks lining the arroyo. That's how the trail got its name—"smooth rock."

The trail suddenly comes out at the water tank where Forest Road 445 leads through the Bernalillo watershed to SR 44. For this hike, it is best if you can arrange to have someone pick you up. The driving distance between the trailhead in Juan Tabo and the trailhead at the watershed is considerable. To get to the Bernalillo side of the trail, take I-25 north to the SR 44–Placitas exit. Follow the highway east about four miles to FR 445, which makes a loop through the watershed (an old Forest Service grazing area, now classified for recreational use); take the *second* junction of SR 44 and FR 445, since it's closer to the trailhead. Follow this dirt road several miles back toward the mountain (it winds its way in several directions and through several arroyos) until you come to the sign marking the left turn onto FR 445A. This short road takes you to the trailhead. Ignore the "No turnaround beyond this point" sign as there is room at the end of the road to turn around. Do be careful of loose sand, however. If you decide to leave a car here, to get back to the trailhead in Juan Tabo Canyon, drive back out to I-25, continue south to the Alameda–Tramway exit and turn left. Continue on Tramway until the junction with FR 333 and follow the previous directions to Piedra Liza Trail.

Approximate hiking time is four to five hours.

EMBUDITO—THREE GUN SPRING

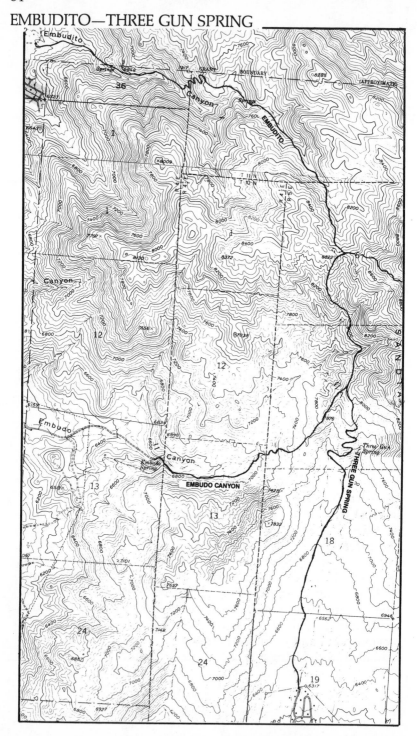

EMBUDITO (#192)—THREE GUN SPRING (#194)
8.5 miles

Embudito Trail is one of the more difficult climbs but also one of the most interesting in the Sandias. As you approach the junction of Embudito and Three Gun Spring Trails, the view of the mountains to the north stretches from Embudito Canyon to the Crest, a unique span visible only from this trail. It makes the hike well worth the effort.

Embudito trailhead is located just east of Glenwood Hills North subdivision. Take Tramway Boulevard north to Montgomery, turn east, and follow Montgomery into Glenwood Hills. Turn left on Glenwood Hills Boulevard and follow it a short way until you see a street which comes to a dead end at the trailhead, which is off to the right. You will see a trail marker and a short wooden stairway that crosses the subdivision fence. A huge water tank sits right next to the trail.

The trail stretches out across the foothills land of chamisa and sage, entering an arroyo for the last quarter mile. Don't make the mistake of following the arroyo up Embudito Canyon; the trail veers off to the left and ascends the north side of the canyon.

The first 1.5 miles are all uphill. The trail climbs through piñon-juniper country, winding through many rocks and boulders. The rock formations along the trail are spectacular; many of the boulders perch precariously (just to the eye—I've never heard of one moving) above the path. The canyon remains visible to the right. In a wet year springs run consistently along its floor.

The trail momentarily levels out just before re-entering the canyon. Box elders denote a spring as you reach the arroyo; go around the rocks to the right and you can soak your head as the water tumbles down the canyon. The trail heads a little way up the canyon floor and then veers off to the left to climb back up to the north bank. Watch for the trail sign (if it's still there).

Once again it's an uphill climb. You begin to see South Peak off to the south. Switchbacks mark the ascent into ponderosa pine, where the trail again levels out before descending into the canyon bottom. Here the trail turns to the south toward South Peak. Follow the canyon bottom for about a quarter of a mile; then cross over to the west side and follow the trail up the canyon. Spruce-fir country begins, and the growth along the path becomes much denser. Springs flow all along the canyon floor to your left.

The trail periodically switchbacks up the canyon, but basically it traverses the west side so that the canyon floor is almost always visible. This is one of the lushest hikes in the mountains; Jacob's ladder, geranium, and vetch line the path. When you start seeing raspberry bushes, the old Embudito shelter site is not far away. The trail opens up at the site and a spur trail crosses over to the spring (or walk across the fallen tree). A log shelter used to sit on the hill above the spring; when the Sandias were declared wilderness in 1978, the shelter was dismantled as there can be no permanent structures in a wilderness area. I usually stop for lunch here. South Peak towers above, and Stellar jays sweep over the spring.

After lunch the hike to the junction with Three Gun Spring Trail is unfortunately uphill, but only for about three-fourths of a mile. This is where a unique view of the Sandias appears. As the trail periodically winds around to the east, through the breaks in the trees you can see the line of the mountains as they head north: Bear Canyon, Pino Canyon, Cañon de Domingo Baca, the Tram, the Crest, and Juan Tabo Ridge. Not only is this a spectacular picture but it shows the true angle of the Sandia range, southeast to northwest.

The trail opens up at the Three Gun Trail junction with a view of South Peak. Another trail also connects here: Oso Pass. This very steep 1.5-mile trail climbs up to South Peak, just to the south of the apex of the mountain, and meets South Crest Trail.

It's all downhill from here. Three Gun Spring Trail starts off to the south. Before heading down the canyon, take a look at the suddenly exposed view to the south: the Manzanitas, the Manzanos, the closer view of Albuquerque, and the route the trail takes down toward civilization. The trail enters Embudo Canyon; the vegetation remains lush since two springs flow across the trail. A little climb brings you up to the saddle between Embudo Canyon and Three Gun Spring. Embudo Trail, described on page 51, leads down into Embudo Canyon; Three Gun Trail continues south toward the town of Carnuel in Tijeras Canyon.

Once the trail leaves the saddle the terrain becomes much more open and, on a hot day, uncomfortable. A series of switchbacks leads down toward the spring; be sure to watch the trail and don't head off down the westernmost arroyo leading out of the canyon. At the end of the last switchback is the spur trail leading up the canyon to Three Gun Spring. Hardwood trees mark the spot. The name "Three Gun" is credited to an old cattle driver who wanted to leave his mark on his territory.

He carved the image of three pistols into the side of a watering trough for his cattle; hence the name "Tres Pistoles," or "Three Gun."

The trail now follows the canyon bottom, winding in and out of the sandy arroyo, which is lined with chamisa. If you're wondering what a small, fenced-off square of land is doing just over to the west of the trail, it's an old Forest Service range management experiment. When grazing was permitted in the canyon, this area was fenced off to measure the cattle's impact on the vegetation. Be careful here; follow the trail rather than the arroyo. The arroyo also comes out in Carnuel, but not where your car will be.

The last leg of the trail comes back out of the arroyo to the east and follows the mesa down to the trailhead. It passes through the forest boundary and one-quarter of a mile later enters the parking area. Some nice big boulders provide welcome shade.

To find Three Gun Spring trailhead, take I-40 east to the Carnuel exit. Turn left at the stop sign; then follow the overpass onto old Highway 66. Take this through town until you see a sign for Monticello Estates subdivision on the left. There is a paved turn into the subdivision (you can cross the highway just east of the turn); follow the road straight up through the development until you see Forest Road 522 marking your turn left. Follow the Forest Road signs into the parking area at the trailhead. Leave one car here and drive back along Tramway to Montgomery to the Embudito trailhead.

Approximate hiking time is six hours.

NORTH CREST (#130) *11 miles*

The sign at the Crest says the distance to Tunnel Spring along North Crest Trail is 11 miles. It certainly seems to be at least 15, but I think that's just my reaction to the last several winding miles above Placitas where the trail seems to go on forever. It was re-routed in the mid-seventies to encompass these last several miles and avoid the steep descent to Tunnel Spring. The old part of the trail heading down the canyon right above the spring still exists, but I wouldn't recommend it.

The first two miles of North Crest Trail to the Cañon del Agua overlook have been described on page 19. From the overlook the trail winds through Gambel oak along the Crest line and then turns slightly east and traverses the mountain to the north Cañon del Agua overlook. Here is where the uppermost roadcut intersects the trail, crossing the mountain from the Crest Highway (State Road 536).

After leaving the overlook the trail begins its long descent through the oak on the east side of the mountains, high above Las Huertas Canyon. The reason for the preponderance of oak over spruce-fir vegetation is fire; it is said that an extensive blaze destroyed the trees here many years ago and that the oak trees have succeeded the burn. This shorter vegetation does provide for panoramic views: the Jemez to the Sangre de Cristos to the Ortiz. The terrain is easy, down the gently sloping east side as the trail winds in long switchbacks toward Tunnel Spring. North Crest is one of the few trails in the Sandias that actually conforms to the 7 percent grade requirement in the Forest Service system. I cross-country skied it once, from the Tram to Placitas, and it was mostly work, not like downhill skiing.

Once through the oak the trail heads into piñon-juniper vegetation and starts to follow the ridgeline again up above Cañon Agua Sarca. There is a stone seat marking the overlook here too—a great place to watch hawks. I've sat for hours amongst the rocks along the ridge watching red-tailed hawks ride the air currents. You can also see some of the old gold and silver mines down in the canyon bottom.

From Agua Sarca overlook it's four more miles. The trail leaves the canyon rim and heads east again toward the village of Placitas. As it passes Cañon Ojo del Orno the old trail straight down to the spring meets the new trail at a barely distinguishable junction. The way down the canyon is very steep and rocky, a treacherous shortcut.

The last two miles of the trail make a loop above Placitas and traverse back to the west toward Tunnel Spring. Be careful not to get off the trail and onto one of the old jeep trails down into the little community of Dome Valley just east of Placitas. As the trail swings west one can see the village and outlying communities. The trail is almost level now, traversing the mountain back to Tunnel Spring. A swimming pool in the back yard of one of the houses in Placitas Heights looks very refreshing.

Finally, around a bend, the big cottonwoods at the spring appear, then the parking lot, then the cold, running stream. This water is potable, piped directly from the underground spring to the outlet here at the trailhead. This water is wonderful tasting, and cool on one's tired feet. Down below the road along the paths are gardens of watercress.

To reach the trailhead at Tunnel Spring take I-25 north to the State Road 44–Placitas exit. Go east about five miles to the Tunnel Spring turnoff. If the sign is down, look for a dirt road to the right just before the highway drops down toward Placitas

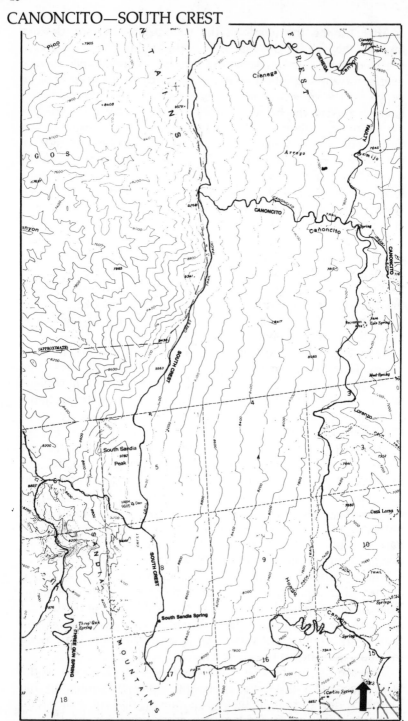

(a row of mailboxes lines the road). Follow Tunnel Spring Road up through the forest boundary, keeping to the left. The road ends in a parking lot just at the trailhead. This hike really necessitates being dropped off at the Crest and then being picked up at Tunnel Spring if a long trip back up the mountain to retrieve a car is to be avoided. If you do leave a car at the Crest, there is a shortcut to get back there from Tunnel Spring. Continue on SR 44 through the village of Placitas; the highway becomes a dirt road as it travels eight miles through Las Huertas Canyon to the junction of the Crest Highway. This is a narrow, winding, busy road, so drive it carefully.

Approximate hiking time is six to seven hours.

CANONCITO (#150)—SOUTH CREST (#130) *12 miles*

There are several routes to South Peak, one of the most isolated and lovely areas in the Sandias. I think the easiest of these routes is up Cañoncito Trail to South Crest Trail, three miles along South Crest Trail to the Peak, and down six miles on the same trail to Canyon Estates. This is truly a hike for the hardy, however, as 12 miles is stretching the limit for a comfortable day hike. That's why most of the hikers you see on South Peak are backpackers.

To get to Cañoncito Trailhead take I-40 to the North 14 exit. It's 3.5 miles to the Cañoncito turnoff; a directional sign on the right-hand side of the road indicates the turn to the town of Cañoncito and the Cole Spring Picnic Ground. Turn left on the dirt road; the Cañoncito trailhead is 1.7 miles in.

The first three-quarters of a mile of this hike to Cañoncito Spring is described on page 27. At the spring Faulty Trail turns south to go five miles to its junction with lower South Crest Trail. Cañoncito Trail, our route, continues up the canyon. It's a moderate climb, although the terrain is quite rocky and hard on the feet. The trail ascends the north side of the canyon through piñon-juniper and ponderosa pine. When it reaches the spruce-fir elevations, the path becomes a little smoother. In August I've seen the beautiful, deep blue western spiderwort growing along the trail.

A switchback leads up to slightly steeper terrain, with more rocks, but the vegetation is lusher, strawberries and fields of purple aster coloring the way. Three-fourths of the way up you will see that many of the Engelmann spruce have dying lower branches. This is due to the spruce budworm, an infestation that has left a swath of dying trees across the east side of the Sandias (visible from the Crest Trail, looking down over Cienega and Cañoncito Canyons). In other areas of the country the official Forest Service policy is to let nature take its course of clearing out diseased vegetation rather than undertaking a controversial spraying program. I believe that the local Forest Service has adopted the same policy with regard to the Sandias.

Near the top of the trail you enter oak and aspen vegetation; the most striking plants are the purple monarda (mint family) and the tall baneberry with its red and white berries (mildly poisonous). The junction with South Crest Trail is amidst oak which prevents any immediate views east or west. To the south is our route, leading nine miles to Canyon Estates; to the north, it's six miles to Sandia Crest.

South Crest Trail is level here, a nice walk south to a western overlook. You will be standing above the Elena Gallegos Land Grant, now a part of the Sandia Wilderness; to the west is Mount Taylor, to the north the Tram, to the south Embudito Canyon. A few more feet down the trail and the eastern view runs from the Sangre de Cristos above Santa Fe to the Gallinas Mountains far to the southeast.

From here the trail begins some uphills over the small peaks which lead up to South Peak. The trail stays just on the east side of the ridgeline, with periodic views west and even more sweeping views to the east. The old Bear Shelter is still standing, just to the right of the trail. The sign there says that Sandia Crest is eight miles away (meaning that you have just walked two miles from the Cañoncito junction) and U.S. Highway 66 is nine miles away (meaning that you have walked one mile from the junction), so it's a guess as to the real distance. I would think that it's about one mile from the junction to the shelter.

From Bear Shelter it's a gradual 1.75-mile uphill climb through aspen groves to South Peak. This is the most beautiful part of the hike. Larkspur, monkshood, and green gentian line the trail under a stately rock formation to the east. As the breezes blow through the thickly growing aspen, we see why "quaking" is part of their name. The trail leads suddenly out of the aspen to a view of South Peak and fields of six-foot-high gentian lying among groves of oak and aspen. On a clear day the view to the east extends from Wheeler Peak above Taos to the Gallinas. You can clearly see the fire lookout on Cedro Peak, down in the Manzanitas.

There is a beautiful aspen grove to the right, at the foot of the peak, the perfect place for lunch. After your meal, if you're feeling energetic (remember, it's six more miles to the trailhead), there's a trail on the south side of the peak that leads up to the top. Walk to the south end of the aspens, then head west along the rock shelf until you pick up the path leading out to the ridgeline. It works its way back north along the limestone rim, scrambling among oak and rocks as it climbs to the highest point of South Peak. The trail is definitely visible once you are up near the ridgeline, so you shouldn't have trouble finding it. Last time I was there, someone had stood a dated piece of wood up in a pile of rocks, marking the top of the peak. The view, along the line of the Sandias running north to the Crest, is unique. The city is stretched out below, a world foreign to this one of mountains and sky, muscles and accomplishment.

Back on the South Crest Trail, the path dips down through an oak and locust grove and emerges into another meadow. Here, at the Deer Pass junction, the Oso Pass Trail leads to your right (northwest) up over the ridge and by a steep 1.5-mile descent to the junction of Embudito and Three Gun Trails (described on page 36). South Crest Trail continues south, six more miles to the trailhead in Canyon Estates (seven miles to U.S. 66). Our trail diverges just beyond the Deer Pass junction, as the old part of the trail heads a little higher across the mountain through an arroyo. The trail was re-routed a few years ago to prevent further erosion in the arroyo; the new trail is the one that dips down through the oak to the east. The two trails merge about three-quarters of a mile later on, before the trail passes by South Sandia Spring. The spring is piped to a box just to the east side of the trail; a spur trail leads into its hidden spot in the oak. Fill your water bottles, as it's a long trek down the mountain.

From the spring the trail quickly heads into drier piñon country. As it follows the ridgeline, a view over into Three Gun Canyon shows the Three Gun Trail heading down from the Embudo saddle. Switchbacks lead southeast from the ridge, through ponderosa pine and over very rocky terrain. The re-routing of the trail can be confusing here, as the trail diverges in several places, but all paths converge eventually. Try to follow the most gradual and least eroded route.

From the switchbacks the trail passes through piñon-juniper country for several miles. The ground vegetation is sparse, but I've seen the purple collomia here, with its dense spike of trumpet-like flowers. The trail descends around the head of a canyon to the junction of Upper Faulty Trail. This can be missed easily, as the trail is not really visible until you walk a few feet off South Crest Trail to the left. It is marked by a square blaze on a tree, however. The Upper Faulty Trail leads northeast to the Faulty

LA LUZ—CREST SPUR—TRAMWAY TRAIL

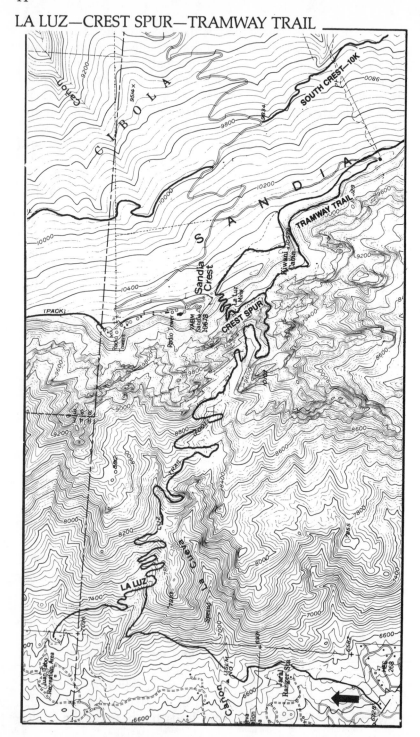

Trail (described on page 29), connecting in a meadow just to the west of the main trail. The South Crest Trail junction with Faulty Trail comes a mile farther south after the Upper Faulty junction. The Faulty Trail junction is marked with a sign. From here it's another mile to the trailhead (described on page 29).

The transportation for this hike is the same as for the Cañon-cito–Faulty–South Crest route.

Approximate hiking time is eight hours.

LA LUZ (#137) *8 miles*
LA LUZ (#137)—CREST SPUR *7.5 miles*
LA LUZ (#137)—TRAMWAY TRAIL (#82) *10 miles*

The La Luz Trail is probably the most well known in the Sandias, and the cause of a lot of problems. Because it's a popular trail, and very accessible to the city, people tackle its eight-mile climb with poor footwear, no water, and little sense of what an eight-mile, 4,000-foot elevation gain means. The La Luz is the scene of at least several search operations each year; somehow someone always manages to lose the well-worn path and end up in Chimney Canyon. An old La Luz route did once ascend Chimney Canyon instead of the present route up Cañon la Cueva, but hardly exists any more. In this trail description I will mention the area where most hikers who lose the trail seem to enter the wrong canyon. At the end of the section I will describe two short trails that hikers can use in conjunction with the La Luz to facilitate transportation arrangements from the Tramway or Sandia Crest.

The trail begins just up the road from the popular Juan Tabo Picnic Ground. Take Tramway Boulevard north from the city, and past the turnoff to the Tram, to the junction with Forest Road 333. Turn right and follow the paved road up into Juan Tabo Canyon, past the turnoff to La Cueva Picnic Ground and the Tierra Monte subdivision, to the entrance to the Juan Tabo Picnic Ground (the second set of pillars). Turn right into the picnic ground and follow the road to its termination at the trailhead. There is plenty of room to park, and a Forest Service sign details distance, estimated hiking time, and safety tips. It's eight miles to the Summit House (the upper Tram terminal) along the La Luz, and 7.5 miles to Sandia Crest using the Crest Spur Trail.

It's piñon-juniper country, with lots of mountain mahogany and gray oak. You can see the radio towers on the Crest and the huge rock pinnacles lining the trail and stretching north through Juan Tabo Canyon. The trail is relatively easy here as it works its way up towards Cañon la Cueva, where the steeper ascent begins. The switchbacks start soon, but the trail remains an easy climb to the junction with Tramway Trail. This trail heads south about two miles to the Tramway, and will be described in detail at the end of this section.

The La Luz continues up the exposed lower part of the canyon into ponderosa pine country. About two miles up is where the old La Luz route heads up Chimney Canyon, misleading some hikers and diverting them from the main trail. You can recognize the place by a sharp bend to the right where the trail crosses a stream. The Chimney Canyon route takes off to the left, and can be followed for a short way before it becomes a bushwhacking ordeal through oak and forest litter.

Back on the main trail the scenery gets more spectacular as you approach the Cañon la Cueva overlook on your right. Follow the little spur trail up to the overlook for an expansive view of the canyon bottom. Behind you loom the granite rock formations that make the west side look so craggy and steep. The Thumb is largest of these pinnacles, and the trail will eventually cross its base.

Farther on, the trail enters upper Cañon la Cueva, marking the steepest part of the climb. The trail follows the north side of the canyon until you pass a small cave on the left and a sign warning you that in wintertime snow can make further travel on the trail extremely difficult. As the trail crosses to the south side of Cañon la Cueva the switchbacks cross the base of the Thumb through the loose rocks of its slopes. It's a difficult climb, but have heart—a respite is in sight.

Once across the talus slopes the switchbacks continue on firmer earth, the path lined with raspberry and thimbleberry bushes. At the north end of one of the uppermost switchbacks is the spur trail leading north to the old La Luz mine, the scene of 19th-century silver mining. Unless someone familiar with the mine shows you the trail, you will have a hard time finding it.

Finally you reach the saddle marking the junction with the Crest Spur Trail. The La Luz continues to the right (southeast) for another 1.25 miles to the Tram. The Crest Spur, to the left, leads half a mile to Sandia Crest.

The La Luz follows the ridgeline of the Sandias several hundred feet below its crest; you can see people standing up on top along the Crest Trail or hear voices drifting down from Kiwanis Cabin. When the bighorn sheep still frequented Kiwanis Meadow, the rock walls above the upper La Luz provided their favorite route down to the Tramway's Tower 2 where they spent a large part of the day.

The first half mile or so along the Crest Trail is a level hike through the trees to the spectacular overlook above Cañon de Domingo Baca where the Tram cars can be seen traveling high over the canyon. The view extends all the way along the ridge of the mountains to South Peak. Back on the trail, locust and oak line the path, so that you sometimes need to bushwhack through the thick growth. The tall climbing figwort is a favorite of the hummingbirds, who divebomb the trail.

Some precipitous spots on the narrow path mark where the sheep descend; a gentle, uphill climb begins for you. The view to the southeast remains open almost all the way to the newly paved, rock-lined path where the trail emerges just north of the High Finance Restaurant. This is where the hang gliders, in all their courageous (?) bravado, jump off the ridge into their flight down the mountain. If you'd rather not jump, you can get back down the mountain by the Tram or by riding the chairlift down to the Ski Area parking lot on the east side. I don't recommend hiking the La Luz up and down in a day (too hard on feet and knees), so I will include several possible alternative routes to connect with car or Tram access.

Approximate time for hiking is five hours.

Crest Spur

If you choose to hike up the La Luz and arrange to have someone pick you up at the Crest, you can detour off the La Luz at the junction with the Crest Spur. This one-half-mile trail leads directly up to Sandia Crest from the seven-mile mark on the La Luz. It's very steep, though, and not a particularly easy end to your hike. (It's hard to imagine people *running* this last half mile after seven previous miles on the La Luz Run.)

The Crest Spur is marked by Forest Service signs at the end of the last La Luz switchback. It heads northwest up through aspen and evergreens just below the exposed limestone rim. The ascent is already steep, but the long, cement stairway ahead begins the *real* climb. The stairs come out along the limestone ledges where you can look for embedded fossils while waiting to catch your breath. Extensive work has been done to secure the trail, but it remains very narrow and slippery due to the soft, eroding lime-stone. There's an overlook on the rocks above Cañon la Cueva where you can look down upon where you've come across the talus slopes of the Thumb. It's only a little farther from here; watch for the switchback heading back south and on up to the stairway at the bottom of the Crest House and parking lot. Watch your footing, too, as there's plenty of loose gravel.

Approximate hiking time is five hours.

Tramway Trail (#82)

If you choose to hike the La Luz and descend the mountain on the Tram, Tramway Trail connects the lower Tram terminal with the La Luz Trail a mile above the trailhead. Tramway Trail trailhead is not easy to find, as it lies right in the middle of Sandia Heights North subdivision and you find yourself walking right next to homes and swimming pools. But there is a Forest Service right-of-way, so use of the trail is legal. (You can skirt the whole problem and set out due north from the Tram, above the houses, and connect with the trail beyond the subdivision.)

To find the trailhead from the Tramway, go down the road past the entry fee station and turn right into Sandia Heights North. Follow Rockridge Drive up into the subdivision until you come to the number 41 address (in large numbers in front of the house). The trailhead is just beyond here to the right, marked by a small trail sign. Follow the path between the houses until you come to the "Entering Cibola National Forest" sign. La Cueva Picnic Ground is three-fourths of a mile and the La Luz Trail two miles.

The trail leaves the houses behind and heads north. All along this trail are various spur trails leading to houses, favorite spots, or shortcuts; follow the basic northerly route that hugs the base of the mountains and you will do fine.

As the trail enters an arroyo you can see the foundation of the old Forest Service ranger station cabin off to the west. There were several of these stations in the Sandias before the existence of the present Ranger Station in Tijeras, when the ranger used to ride his horse through the mountains on patrol, from cabin to cabin. Another cabin existed where the Snowplay Area is today in Capulin Picnic Ground.

The trail is fairly level along here but becomes more uphill as you approach La Cueva Picnic Ground. The La Cueva Trail leads a quarter mile west to the picnic ground; a Forest Service sign says it's 1.25 miles more to the La Luz Trail. There's a great view of the Crest from here; you can look with satisfaction at where you've been.

It's all uphill from here, above Tierra Monte subdivision (the swimming pools visible from the trail are torture on a hot day) and northwest along the ridge to La Luz Trail. Several old trails take off from this ridge heading due east up into Cañon la Cueva. These are old La Luz routes that bypass the switchbacks but are not recommended. Tramway Trail comes around the ridge and levels off as it meets the La Luz in the canyon bottom. Its an easy one-mile hike back down to the La Luz trailhead.

The La Luz–Tramway hike is definitely an all-day excursion, with a diversionary ride down on the Tram, so take your time and enjoy this mountain experience.

OSHA LOOP 2.6 miles

Osha Loop Trail is a difficult one to find and follow; consequently, Cañon Osha remains one place where the Sandia bears live in relative peace. Please, when hiking this trail, be aware that you are invading another creature's territory and make your visits to the spring short and sweet.

The loop begins at Cañon Media on the 10K Trail, traverses north to Cañon Osha, then west (uphill) to the junction of North Crest Trail. You can hike into Cañon Media along the northern part of 10K Trail (described in Section 1). Take the spur trail down to the spring (to the right at the misplaced "Osha Canyon" sign). Just before you reach the spring you'll come across a square shallow hole in the ground, walled with fallen logs. There's some speculation as to the origin of this obviously man-made structure; my own guess is that it's a hunting blind, placed near the spring to catch the animals when they come to drink (definitely illegal!). Osha Loop Trail begins to the left (north), just above the blind. This one-mile trail from Cañon Media to Cañon Osha is primitive and difficult to follow in spots. The Sandia Wildlife volunteer group has marked the trail with cairns, but those don't always remain in place. If you find yourself off the trail, backtrack to the last cairn and start again until you find the path.

At the junction with Osha Spring Trail, Osha Spring is 0.3 miles north (to the right, downhill). If you decide to take a side trip to the spring, follow the trail downhill until you come to the junction with an old jeep road. To the right, the road travels east, down the mountain, to Las Huertas Road. It's a long, hot, rocky hike down the jeep trail and not recommended to the leisurely hiker. To the left along the jeep road is the spur trail down to Osha Spring. The trail descends the side of the canyon steeply and opens up in a meadow at the spring. In a wet year water will be trickling down over the white rocks into the locust and gooseberry bushes where the wildlife tank is hidden. When heading into the bushes be sure to make plenty of noise so that whatever creature may be there has time to retreat farther into the foliage. To the north of Osha Spring, hidden in more gooseberry bushes, are the foundations of some old homesteading cabins.

Back at the junction of the trail coming over from Cañon Media you will find that the Osha Loop Trail continues up the mountain (to the left) toward the roadcut. There are several switchbacks where you can easily lose the trail, so watch for the tree blazes and the most heavily traveled path. At the roadcut (the same one that 10K Trail crosses further south) walk south until you can see a trail heading up the ridge into the trees. This short spur trail leads up to North Crest Trail, just north of Cañon del Agua overlook. To complete the loop, it's two miles south on North Crest Trail to Sandia Crest (the first leg of the hike described on page 19.

To hike into Osha Loop Trail along 10K Trail and back to the Crest along North Crest Trail allow yourself approximately six hours.

OSHA LOOP

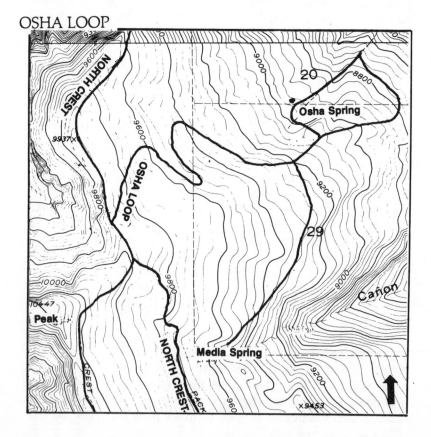

EMBUDO CANYON *3.25 miles*

The Embudo Canyon Trail was completed in 1984. Over the years many hikers have followed their own routes up Embudo Canyon to the junction with Three Gun Trail. Now the Forest Service has marked a trail to guide hikers on a 10- to 15-percent grade up the canyon on a route designed to minimize erosion.

The trailhead is just west of the city open space area near the city water tank at Embudo Canyon. Take Menaul Boulevard east to Rio Bonito to the designated parking area. The trail leads 3.25 miles up the southeast side of Embudo Canyon, crossing the canyon bottom once and passing the springs and small waterfall flowing in the lower part of the canyon. With an average grade of only 10 to 12 percent, the trail is geared to the casual hiker.

As the trail turns and climbs up the east side of the canyon, the grade increases to 15 percent at some places. Embudo Trail comes to a junction with Three Gun Trail on the saddle where Three Gun crosses the Embudo drainage. To the right (south) Three Gun Trail continues several miles to the trailhead in Carnue . To the left (north) Three Gun climbs to the junction with Oso Pass and Embudito Trails (described on pages 35-37).

Approximate hiking time is three hours.

EMBUDO CANYON

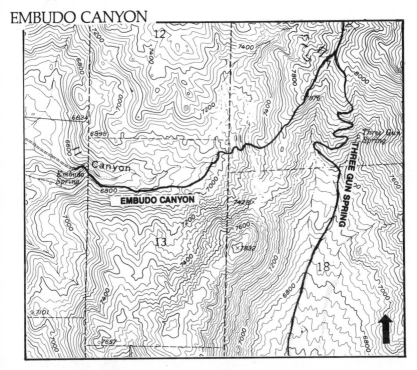

PART III.
HIKING TRAILS
IN THE MANZANO MOUNTAINS

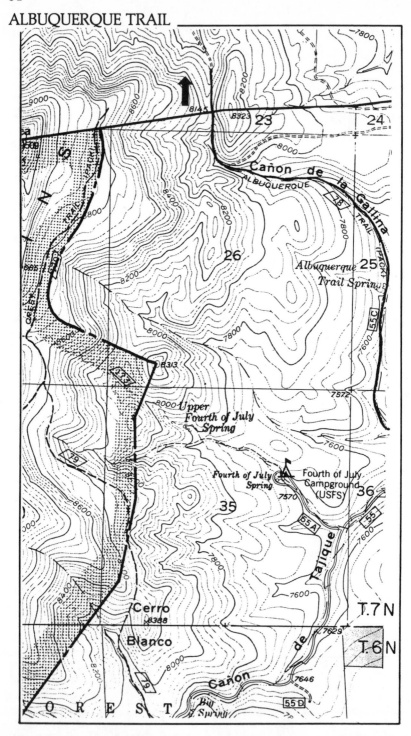

ALBUQUERQUE TRAIL (#78) *1.7 miles*

This short, easy trail is at the extreme north end of the Manzanos, beginning on Forest Road 55 and terminating at the forest boundary. In the same area of the mountains as the famous Fourth of July Trail, Albuquerque Trail is a beautiful fall hike through stands of Rocky Mountain maple. There is no connecting trail to make a loop; the round-trip route is 3.4 miles.

Take I-40 east to the South 14–Tijeras exit and drive 31 miles to the junction of FR 55 in the town of Tajique. It's 6.7 miles west on FR 55 to the Albuquerque trailhead sign, and another quarter-mile north on a narrow, primitive road to the trailhead itself. You can leave your car at the turnoff on FR 55 or drive into any of several camping areas in meadows adjacent to the trailhead.

The trail is a continuation of the road until you reach the spring, about a quarter of a mile up. Then it narrows to a path through Transition zone vegetation of oak and ponderosa pine. There are some magnificent pines here, fully matured with red-colored bark and a sweet, vanilla smell. It's an easy climb into the stands of Rocky Mountain maple.

The upper part of the trail is slightly steeper as the vegetation changes to spruce-fir. Bear to the left at the junction of an old trail turning right. At a fence line the trail turns to the right and ascends 100 yards or so to the forest boundary fence. To the north is the Isleta Indian Reservation and a view of the Sandia Mountains. The trail terminates here (an old road descends the Isleta side); estimated hiking time for a round trip is two to three hours.

FOURTH OF JULY (#173)—CREST (#170)— CERRO BLANCO (#79) *4.5 miles*

This is the famous hike of the fall season, when the Rocky Mountain maple turns brilliant red up and down the canyons in a spectacle of color. It's a relatively short hike, making a loop up Fourth of July Canyon, south along the Manzano Crest Trail, and down Cerro Blanco Trail back to Fourth of July Campground.

To reach the trailhead in Fourth of July Campground take I-40 east to the South 14–Tijeras exit. Stay on South 14 for 31 miles to the town of Tajique. The turnoff to the campground is posted; Forest 55, a dirt road, leads seven miles toward the mountains. Turn right into the campground (also posted); the trailhead is just to the right in the parking area

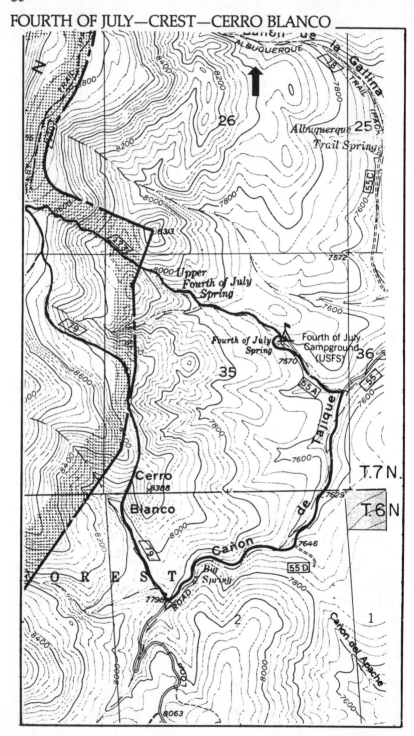

at the end of the road as it begins a loop back out.

Fourth of July is a primitive trail. It follows the canyon on the east side of the Manzanos. Springs are usually running along the canyon bottom, making this a wet hike. The maples start almost immediately, mixing with the green and gold of pine and oak. It's 1.3 miles to the junction with the Manzano Crest Trail.

The first half of the hike is a modest climb up through maples, basically following along the bottom of the canyon. At Fourth of July Spring, where the trail steepens considerably, there are actually three routes to the Crest Trail. The official Forest Service trail, re-routed in 1983, turns left (south) to traverse the mountain over to a junction with the Cerro Blanco Trail below the Crest. The re-routing was done to create a route causing less erosion than the two already existing paths to the Crest. The main erosion culprit is the route that continues directly up the canyon, along the steep and rocky canyon bottom. This way is the quickest but toughest route to the top.

Our hike follows the third route, north out of the canyon bottom and up over the ridge to the Crest Trail. Watch for the tree blazes that guide you in a northwesterly direction through the spruce-fir vegetation and into the oak on top. The trail emerges into a large, beautiful meadow clustered with oaks just on the east side of the Crest. The trail that ascends straight up the canyon bottom emerges in the same meadow, a little farther south. Despite the official Forest Service re-routing, I believe the northern route described here provides the best route for the hiker. The erosion problems along this path are less severe than in the canyon-bottom trail, and the meadow must not be missed. It's a real Alpine setting with a magnificent view and lovely oak stands providing shade and respite. It's the perfect place for lunch.

Cut across the meadow toward the ridgeline to find the Crest Trail. To the north the trail leads to its origin near Mosca Peak. To the south it follows the ridgeline all the way to Manzano Peak. Before continuing south, follow the spur trail west to the overlook. Here the Ojito Trail, a primitive 4.8-mile descent of the west side, meets the Crest Trail. The view provides the same spectacular panorama of the Rio Grande valley as is seen from the Sandias, only farther south. Belen and Los Lunas are the cities below. Go all the way out onto the rock ledge below the trail for a view of more maples down in the canyon below.

SPRUCE SPRING—CREST—RED CANYON

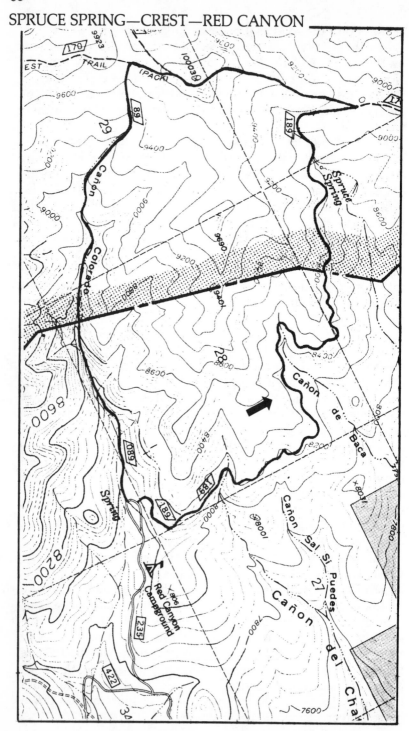

It's a short, easy walk along the Crest Trail to the junction with Cerro Blanco Trail. The terrain is very similar to that of the Crest Trail in the Sandias: oaks line the path following the ridgeline south. Cerro Blanco, the first trail descending east from the Crest Trail, is also easy, leading 1.5 miles down the canyon where it connects with FR 55. There are a few steep switchbacks near the top, but the trail quickly levels out as it descends the side of the canyon, affording views of the maple-red canyons and peaks to the south. If you look closely the fire lookout on Capilla Peak can be seen.

At the junction with FR 55 a cool stream provides respite from the heat. To the left is the way back to the entrance to Fourth of July Campground; to the right (south), FR 55 leads to the town of Torreón. Watch for the traffic coming in both directions. It's about a one-mile hike back to the entrance of the campground, then another quarter-mile to the trailhead. A word of warning about FR 55: during the rainy season it becomes impassable, from both Tajique and Torreón. Plan this hike for the early summer months or October when the leaves have turned. You can call the Mountainair Ranger Station to find out when the best days for color viewing will be.

Approximate hiking time is four hours.

SPRUCE SPRING (#189—CREST (#170)— RED CANYON (#89) *7 miles*

This system of trail makes a complete loop, beginning and ending in Red Canyon Campground near the town of Manzano. It's a beautiful hike, offering varied views, Alpine meadows, lush vegetation, and moderate hiking.

Take I-40 to South 14, and it's 39 miles to Manzano. Drive through town to the junction with Forest Road 253, which leads over six miles of good gravel road to Red Canyon Campground, a quiet place (at least during the week), thoughtfully laid out by the Forest Service. Both Spruce Spring and Red Canyon trailheads are marked.

Spruce Spring Trail is about a mile longer than Red Canyon Trail (3.5 miles compared with 2.4), but it conforms to a nine-percent grade and is a much easier ascent. The lower part of the trail reminds me of Cañoncito Trail, winding through ponderosa pine and magnificent alligator juniper. The trail heads northwest out of the campground, over toward Cañon del Chato, where it climbs around the head of the canyon on its way up the mountain. The vegetation quickly becomes lush;

raspberries and strawberries abound, and if you look closely, you will spot the first of many fairy slipper orchids.

The trail continues northwest toward the head of the next canyon, Cañon de los Pinos Reales. Just past the three-mile marker a spur trail leads off to the right to Spruce Spring. Then it's a short distance to the top of the climb, a big Alpine meadow marking the crest. Stands of oak and thick, stunted-looking ponderosa provide shelter and lunch spots. At the top of the meadow you can see the west face of the Manzanos and look west down to the Rio Grande valley and north along the line of the mountains past Capilla Peak to Mosca Peak. The Manzano Crest Trail continues north to its junction with Trigo Trail and beyond that to its inception at the forest boundary.

A trail sign points the way south along the Crest Trail to Red Canyon Trail. Before starting out spend some time enjoying the meadow and refreshing yourself since it's mostly an uphill climb along the Crest as it ascends Gallo Peak. The trail starts out along the fence right at the Crestline and then climbs on the east side through the vegetation. As you near the crest of Gallo Peak several little spur trails lead out to spectacular views of the west side of the Manzanos.

About halfway along the 1.25-mile hike to Red Canyon the trail levels out. It's obvious that the Manzano Crest Trail isn't used as much as the Sandia Crest Trail; it's much less worn and more overgrown. The Red Canyon–Crest Trail junction is in a meadow, a good place to rest before the fairly steep descent into Red Canyon. A trail sign in the middle of the meadow marks the junction.

Red Canyon Trail is not a good one for running shoes; its steep and rocky terrain is hard on feet that have already hiked five miles, but the beauty of the canyon compensates for any discomfort. About one-third of the way down a spring bubbles out into a mountain stream and provides variety as the stream crosses and re-crosses the trail innumerable times. I have seen patches of orchids alongside the stream—thirty orchids at a time, a rare occurrence. Red and gold columbines also flourish, along with figwort, violets, strawberries, and valerian.

The trail becomes quite rocky halfway down, as the canyon narrows and is closed in by sheer rock walls on either side. You must scramble over the stream in some places as it almost obliterates the trail, but the canyon is so narrow that there's little chance of losing the way. Several fairly large waterfalls come cascading down beside the trail, and butterflies cluster about the spray.

The trail levels out near the end as it emerges from the rocks. A boundary sign marks the end of the wilderness, and a fence and gate show the entry to the campground.

Approximate hiking time is six hours.

OX CANYON (#190)—CREST (#170)—
RED CANYON (#89) 7.5-9 *miles*

This is another hike that can be made from a base in Red Canyon Campground. Ox Canyon Trail climbs 3.5 miles up Ox Canyon (south of Red Canyon) to the Manzano Crest Trail, where it's a 1.5-mile hike north over to Red Canyon and back down into the campground.

To get to Red Canyon Campground, take I-40 east to the South 14–Tijeras exit and drive 39 miles to the town of Manzano. Take Forest Road 253 for six miles west to the campground. Ox Canyon trailhead starts from a road off Forest Road 422, which is two miles east of Red Canyon Campground on FR 253. There's a sign at the junction of the two roads; FR 422 branches to the south. It's almost a four-wheel-drive road, although a pickup truck driven by a brave soul can make it to the trailhead. Keep to the right as you travel the first two miles to the sign which points the direction to Ox Canyon Trail. FR 422 continues to the left; the road to the trailhead is to the right. The road worsens considerably here so it's a good place to start to hike if you don't have four-wheel drive. The sign is misleading, indicating that the trailhead is three miles away. Actually it's only about 1.5 miles.

The walk to the trailhead is easy but a bit confusing with all the logging roads that crisscross the area. Stay on the road until you come to the junction with a "Primitive Road" (it is classified as such by a sign) and turn left toward the mountains. You'll cross a logging road a little farther on, but keep straight ahead (basically northwest). The road is overgrown here, but still clearly visible. At the next junction with a logging road that makes a sharp left, stay to your right until you get to the trailhead sign. The road has a north and a south branch here; take the south branch, right next to the sign, for a quarter of a mile until another sign marks the entrance of the trail into the trees. It's a 3.5-mile climb up to the Crest Trail.

Ox Canyon is a beautiful, wide canyon spreading out into two forks at its head. The trail (blazed by old Forest Service cuts in trees) crosses to the north side of the canyon for the first half of the hike, ascending through columbine, raspberry bushes,

OX CANYON—CREST—RED CANYON

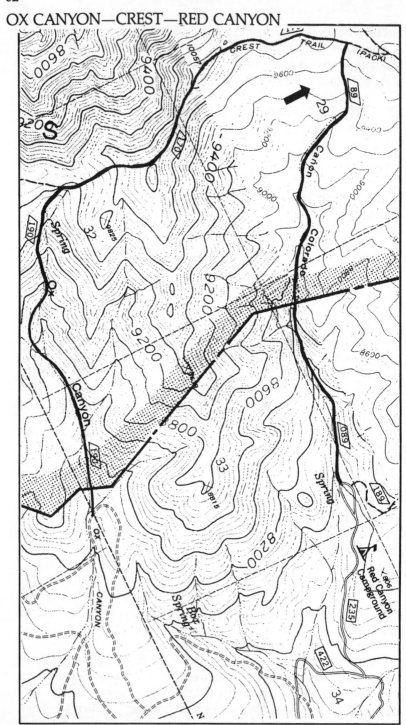

four-foot-high figwort, and even some low-country aspen.

Switchbacks begin over a rockslide area and continue up the north side until views open up for a panorama of the Estancia valley. Even with the switchbacks the trail is relatively easy, at about the same level of difficulty as Spruce Spring Trail. Two-thirds of the way up the trail crosses a spring; an old log bridge has fallen into the water but the crossing remains easy. Many bluebells grow along the stream banks; I've eaten strawberries by the second week of July.

The trail then switchbacks up the ridge between the upper forks of the canyon through stands of aspen and open views to the east. It then heads up the south fork until it switchbacks again over to the north fork—watch the tree blazes carefully to follow the turns. The last leg of the trail is back on the ridge, through aspen and up to the clearing of the Crest Trail.

The signs at the junction have been broken loose from their posts but can be found lying on the ground. To the south along the Crest Trail, it's one mile to the junction with the Kayser Mill Trail, an east-side trail ascending from Kayser Mill Forest Road 275 (described in Section 6). To the north it's a 1.5-mile hike along the Crest Trail to Red Canyon.

At the junction of Ox Canyon and Crest Trails, there is a slightly obscured view through the trees to the west. The Crest Trail leads northwest up through a meadow to the ridgeline and a clearer view down over Cañon Monte Largo to the Rio Grande valley. This is pretty much the last of the uphill as the trail drops over to the west side across the head of the canyon.

Back on the east side the trail continues to the junction with the Salas Trail (#184), which leads west 7.75 miles down to John F. Kennedy Campground on Forest Road 33 at the west foot of the Manzanos. The Crest Trail continues for a half-mile more to the junction with Red Canyon Trail. The 2.5-mile hike down Red Canyon into the campground is described in Section 2.

This is a 7.5-mile hike if you drive right to the Ox Canyon trailhead; if you walk from the first trail sign it's nine miles.

Approximate hiking time is five to six hours.

CAPILLA PEAK—CREST TRAIL (#170) *6 miles*

There is really no loop hike that can be made from Capilla Peak Campground in a day, but since it's such a nice place to camp, I'll describe a round-trip route south along the Crest Trail that makes an interesting day's excursion.

To get to Capilla Peak Campground, take South 14 to the town of Manzano, then turn west on Forest Road 245 (across

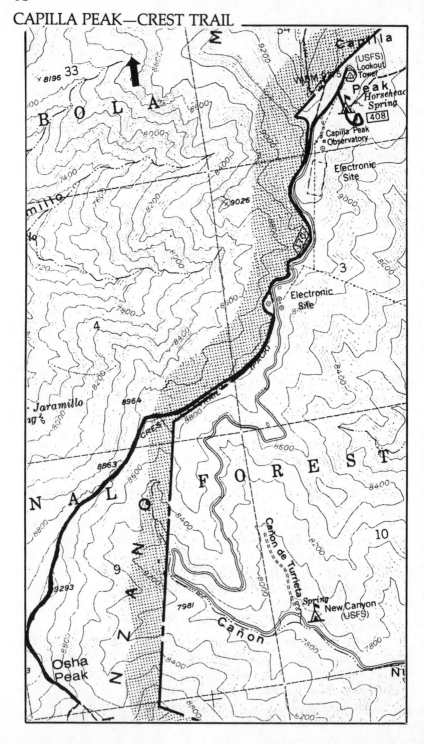

the road from the church). Capilla Peak is nine miles up on a pretty good dirt road. You'll pass New Canyon Campground on the way up, another nice place to camp. An old trail, marked by a tree blaze, begins just beyond the campground and ascends the south side of the canyon in a steep climb to the junction of the Crest Trail and Trigo Canyon Trail. FR 245 intersects the Crest trail at the microwave towers; the road continues to the right another mile to the campground and fire lookout. The Crest Trail heading north is just below the lookout, next to the road.

To begin the hike you can either leave your car in the campground and walk back to the trailhead along the road or park your car at the trailhead (be sure not to block access to the microwave buildings). The trail begins just over the hill south of the towers. A sign says it's three miles south to the junction with Trigo Canyon Trail and five miles to Spruce Canyon.

This hike is an up-and-down one, along narrow ridges, through meadows, and over peaks to the junction with Trigo Canyon Trail. The ridgeline of the Manzanos is narrow along the beginning of the hike, affording views to east and west. After going up and down through ponderosa pine, the trail climbs up onto the peak north of Osha, then down into a saddle between the two peaks. This is one of the few places in the Manzanos or Sandias where I have seen the beautiful fairy primrose; it grows in the rock crevices above the trail, along with the rock-loving alumroot.

In the saddle, a little spur trail, marked by a cairn, leads downhill to the west. It's only a few-hundred yards along this trail to a beautiful mountain meadow, the perfect place for lunch. In the northeast corner of the meadow are the remains of an old cabin and just below that, a seep spring. The person who showed me the meadow referred to it as the old "sheepherder's meadow," but who built the old cabin is a mystery since it's on Forest land.

The Crest Trail continues south around the west side of Osha Peak, then switchbacks down to the saddle where it intersects with Trigo Canyon Trail. It's back into ponderosa and piñon country here, where the rangeland fence cuts across the mountain. If you arrange for transportation you can continue to the west along the four-mile Trigo Canyon Trail to John F. Kennedy Campground, a reasonable day's hike (remember, it takes about three hours by car to get around the mountain from the west to the east side). The Crest Trail continues through the gate in the rangeland fence and on toward Spruce Canyon Trail. Right

BOSQUE—CREST—TRAIL CANYON

before the trail sign is the trail leading down to New Canyon Campground, another possible route back to FR 245. The trail-head is marked on a tree by blazes which look like a face.

For the round-trip excursion of six miles you should turn back toward Capilla at the point where Crest Trail intersects Trigo Canyon Trail.

Approximate hiking time for the round-trip excursion is five hours.

BOSQUE (#174)—CREST (#170)—
TRAIL CANYON (#176) 7-9 miles

This is a beautiful loop of trails including one of the most spectacular sections of the Crest Trail, high above Comanche Canyon. Bosque and Trail Canyon Trails begin on Forest Road 55, about two miles apart. If you hike the road between the two trailheads, the entire loop is nine miles. If you arrange to be picked up, or leave two cars, you can cut the mileage to seven.

Bosque trailhead is just about equidistant from the towns of Torreón and Tajique on FR 55. If you're coming from the south on South 14, then turn left onto FR 55 in Torreón and travel 8.5 miles to the trail. This way you will pass Trail Canyon trailhead; there is no sign marking the trail so it's best to start this hike from Bosque trailhead. I will describe the Trail Canyon trailhead as best I can at the end of this section.

Bosque Trail, which reaches the Crest in about two miles, starts out as a wide, rocky path up through Gambel oak and quickly becomes quite steep. About three-quarters of a mile up, a switchback momentarily levels the trail, and one of the first of many views south to Capilla Peak opens up. The trail then ascends the north side of the canyon through more oak and occasional ponderosa pine.

Cave Spring, a watering tank for cattle, can be seen down in the canyon bottom. Various spur trails lead down to the water. A few feet past the first sighting of the spring a short spur trail leads to the right, up to a cave in the canyon wall. I don't know how far back it leads, but it seems to turn and head back into the rock wall.

You are on private land now, a half-section that originally belonged to the Fromwalt family, whose old homestead cabin still sits on top of the Manzanos near the Creat Trail. This is a good place to eat lunch after conquering the Bosque Trail (don't look forward to it as a shelter during a rainstorm though—it's just a ruin).

Farther on up the trail, large stands of oak and New Mexico locust (the largest I've ever seen in the Manzanos or Sandias) divide the canyon into small meadows. The trail emerges into a larger meadow just below the Crest Trail and continues southwest through the clearing (it's hard to see a path here). It turns south very soon, by an old trail marker, and comes up along the ridgeline. The view to the northeast makes the hard climb up Bosque worth every breath: Cerro Blanco is the closest mountain to the northeast; Mosca and Guadalupe Peaks mark the Forest boundary; and the Sandias define the northernmost horizon.

The junction with the Crest Trail is just ahead. Our hike continues south along the Crest to Trail Canyon Trail, but a detour north to the aspen grove just above the trail will take you to the old Fromwalt cabin. Walk north along the Crest Trail until the aspens are above you, then turn west and you'll spot the cabin and several other structures nearby. It's hard to imagine anyone spending the winter up here, but according to Mrs. Fromwalt of Tajique, a woman in her nineties, her family did just that. The only living beings up here now are cows, who belong to the current owner of the mountain land.

It's hard to get a western view from here because of the dense oak west of the aspen grove, but back out on the Crest Trail heading south views become panoramic. A little way past the Bosque Trail junction, signs give the mileage to various trails. Comanche Canyon Trail, which descends the west side to John F. Kennedy Campground, is three miles south. At the same place Trail Canyon Trail intersects the Crest Trail from the east. Encino Trail is only 200 feet south, but this hard-to-find trail descending the west face to Comanche Canyon is not maintained and seldom used. Capilla Peak is eight miles south, Cerro Blanco Trail four miles north, and Mosca Peak is two miles beyond that.

The Crest Trail south is downhill through open meadows; cairns mark the barely discernable path. The view south is across Capilla Peak to Gallo Peak, above Red Canyon. Both Trail Canyon to the east and Comanche Canyon to the west are visible as the trail follows the ridgeline toward the saddle between the two. This is a truly remarkable stretch of trail, right along the top of the little-known but awesome Manzano Mountains.

Watch for the cairn that marks the trail as it drops off to the east through a thick growth of oak. You come out on a narrow ridge above Comanche Canyon. Sit on the rocks above this huge canyon and enjoy your last view of the great west-facing canyons. There's supposed to be an old gold mine down there somewhere, but I doubt that there's enough gold left to make a search for it worthwhile.

From here the trail switcbacks down to a saddle, then up onto the last ridge before the Trail Canyon junction. The path is overgrown with oak so shorts aren't recommended. It's also very rocky, so you need boots rather than running shoes. A switch-back leads you back down the ridge to the saddle between Comanche and Trail Canyons. It's a long eight-mile trek down Comanche Canyon Trail to John F. Kennedy Campground and an easy two-mile hike down Trail Canyon Trail to FR 55. Capilla Peak is three miles farther south on the Crest Trail (all uphill).

Trail Canyon Trail reminds me of Cerro Blanco Trail, farther north. It's lined with Rocky Mountain maple, making it spectac-ular in the fall. A wide, easy path goes down through the maples into oak and ponderosa pine. Watch for the re-routing of the trail north of where the original trail continues down Trail Can-yon. Apparently some problems arose with the trail crossing private land, so the Forest Service re-routed the lower trail over to the old Diablo Canyon Trail. The last time I was there, yellow flagging guided the way down. The new route climbs a ridge to the north above Trail Canyon, then heads down to FR 55 through another swath of maple. It emerges onto the road a mile farther north than the old trail. There's a pull-off area here, marked by part of an old road, and an "Entering Private Land" sign on the fence just north of the trailhead. It's two miles north along FR 55 to the Bosque trailhead where you started.

Approximate hiking time for the seven-mile hike is six hours; add an hour if you make the nine-mile trek.

COTTONWOOD (#73)—KAYSER MILL (#80)— PINE SHADOW (#170A) *9 miles*

This is the southernmost trail loop in the Manzanos, Pine Shadow being the last leg of the Crest Trail as the latter heads south into Priest Canyon. It's a long, hot hike so be sure to take plenty of water.

Cottonwood Trail begins off Forest Road 422, one-half mile beyond Pine Shadow trailhead, so this system of trails can be hiked as a complete loop. Take U.S. 60 west out of Mountainair, 13 miles to the junction with FR 422 (marked by a small, white road sign). Turn north on FR 422 (a good dirt road) and go 11 miles to the Pine Shadow trailhead. You'll pass several ranches and the ruins of an adobe cabin which names Priest Canyon. The Spanish priest who lived here is said to have been murdered

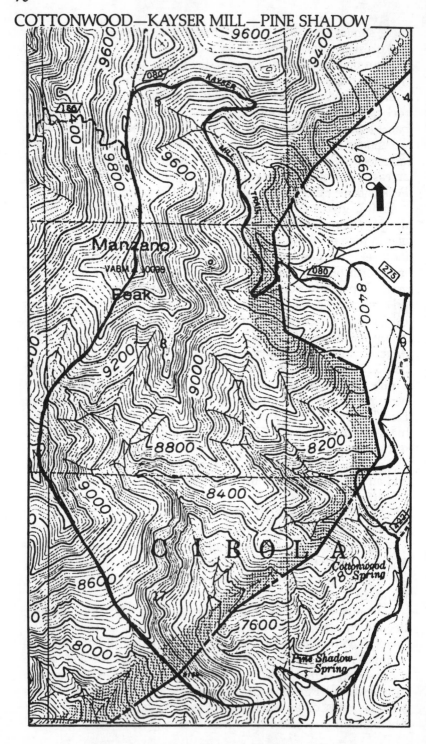

for his silver by a band of outlaws during colonial days. The trailhead is marked by a sign (which calls the trail Crest Trail); there are camping areas on both sides of the road where you can park your car.

Cottonwood trailhead is a half mile farther north on FR 422. The sign there tells you that the trail goes 1.5 miles to the junction with Forest Road 275 and another quarter mile along FR 275 to the Kayser Mill Trail. The trail takes off on the west side of the road by a springbox; a directional sign points the way down into the canyon where the trail then turns and climbs north up the east side of the canyon. It's a very steep climb up onto the ridge where the trail momentarily levels out before heading back up over another ridge. This is all piñon-juniper and pine country, so it's a hot hike up to the high country on Kayser Mill Trail. At the one-mile marker the trail descends to the junction with FR 275. Turn left (west) and walk along the road a quarter of a mile to the Kayser Mill Trailhead. FR 275 is negotiable with a high-clearance vehicle in good weather, so this hike can actually begin at the Kayser Mill trailhead if someone will drop you off there.

Kayser Mill Trail, 1.5 miles in length, is less steep than Cottonwood Trail and takes you quickly up into the high country of spruce and fir. Raspberries proliferate. At the wilderness boundary sign the trail turns south for a quarter of a mile; then switchbacks take you north across a fork of Kayser Mill Canyon. As the trail climbs around the head of the canyon, a spring can be found down to your right in the canyon bottom. By July and August it's usually only a trickle, so don't rely on it for water. I've seen monkshood and primrose growing here, two of the more unusual Manzano flowers.

As the trail comes around the head of the canyon it crosses a large rockslide, then switchbacks up to the top of the ridge into a meadow. There is an old trail marker here, at the bottom of the meadow where Kayser Mill emerges, but the trailhead would be hard to find from the Crest Trail since there is no path through the meadow and the old trail sign is not visible.

The Crest Trail here is not very visible, but it's clear enough to follow. Turn south, and it's about a 200-yard climb to a great view of both the east and the west sides of the mountains. The distance to Manzano Peak is about three-fourths of a mile, mostly level hiking, as the trail crosses over to the east side of the ridge. At the junction with Pine Shadow Trail, a quarter-mile spur trail leads up to the top of Manzano Peak, the highest in the Manzano range. There's a box on a post there, with a notebook so that hikers will sign their names, registering their achievement.

The Pine Shadow Trail, 5.5 miles down to FR 422, starts out west around Manzano Peak. It's still nice and lush up here, with more raspberries to pick. As the trail goes across the head of the canyon, the view opens up to the south, showing the last line of the Manzano peaks across U.S. 60. After the trail crosses through an old burn area, be careful not to miss the switchback down to the west. From here across the head of the canyon (one of the subsidiaries of Priest Canyon) the trail is very rocky and steep. You're getting into lower country now, piñon-juniper, and because the trail is exposed to the south, it can get very hot; it reminds me of the South Crest Trail in the Sandias coming down to the junction with Faulty.

The last several miles of the trail wind down to the southeast; glimpses of FR 422 show you your destination. You can see the red mesa stretching down Priest Canyon along the road. The trail crosses the wilderness boundary, goes through a cattle gate, and arrives at the sign marking the trail's end. The road is just a hundred yards beyond.

Approximate hiking time is seven hours.

West Side Hikes

All the Manzano hikes described so far have been on the east side of the mountains or along the Crest Trail where complete loops or easy car shuttling is possible. The trails on the west side of the mountains are mostly too long and too distant from each other to make complete loops practical. I will list the west-side trails individually, with a brief description of terrain and location. If you choose to backpack and spend several days on these trails, then loops can be made without transportation problems since three of the trails originate in John F. Kennedy Campground. Or they can be ascended and descended in one day, but I don't recommend it; hiking should be for fun, not a marathon event.

TRIGO CANYON TRAIL (#182) *4 miles*

This trail is the shortest of the west-side hikes and can be climbed up and down in a day. It begins in John F. Kennedy Campground, which is well off the beaten track in the western foothills of the Manzanos. Take I-25 or State Road 47 south to Belen; the dirt road leading into the campground is several miles south of Belen on State Road 6, the road to Mountainair. Two miles past the junction of SR 47 and SR 6 (going south on SR 6) is a set of adobe-colored pillars on the left-hand side of the road. They mark a dirt road which leads eight miles east to Forest Road 33, which leads in turn to the campground. The eight-mile road is not in great shape, however, and there is another dirt road, several miles farther south on SR 6 that also leads to FR 33. This alternative road is also marked by pillars, and by a Forest Service sign, "John F. Kennedy Campground 19 miles." Follow the road to the junction with FR 33, which heads back north into the campground.

The trailhead is at the east end of the campground through a gate (usually unmarked). This is a beautiful hike for the fall, as the trail follows streambeds almost all the way to the top and is colored by the yellows and browns and reds of oak, willow, elm, and Virginia creeper.

The trail begins as a wide path lined with alligator juniper and Apache plume. The canyon narrows as you reach the stream-bed, and the trail crosses the stream many times during the ascent. Huge, layered rock formations form the canyon walls as you pass through stands of willow, elm, and box elder. The stream is usually quite full, with pools and waterfalls creating a humid environment. Evening primrose, strawberry, and mint grow in the moist soil along the streambed.

After a while the canyon opens up and you can see up toward the crest. The trail enters the south fork of the canyon, following another spring. A short, steep climb brings you to a junction; stay to the right, following the stream.

The trail leaves the canyon bottom for a while and begins a steep climb up the south side. The terrain levels out again at the streambed. There's an obvious camping place in a stand of spruce and fir next to a shallow cave. Keep following the stream on the north side as it crosses a rock ledge; then it will re-cross to the south side of the canyon where it meets an old fenceline and turns south to follow another spring. At the waterfall it switch-backs to the north, up the ridge. A spur trail leads off to the left to an overlook above the canyon.

From here it's another steep climb until the western rock face of Osha Peak comes into view. The trail leads up through stands of oak and aspen into the mixed conifers just below the Crest. The last half mile is through dryer country as the springs are left behind. The trail emerges at the Manzano Crest Trail. To the north the Crest Trail climbs Osha Peak and continues on to Capilla Peak (described in Section 4); to the south it heads toward Spruce Spring Trail. The old trail into New Canyon Campground also emerges at the Trigo–Crest Trail junction.

TRIGO CANYON TRAIL

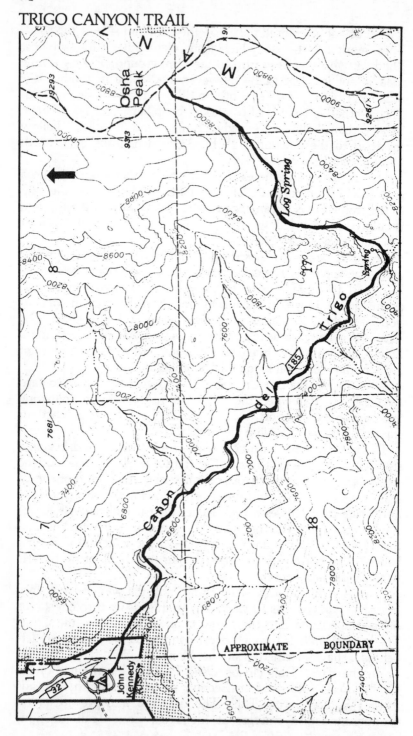

There's no view here in any direction, so the hike's end is a little anticlimactic, but the beauty of the route should compensate for this.

Approximate hiking time for going up and down this trail is five hours.

SALAS TRAIL (#184) *7.75 miles*

This west-side hike begins at John F. Kennedy Campground and intersects the Crest Trail half a mile south of Red Canyon Trail. It's named for the Old Forest Service outpost at the foot of Cañon de Salas where the trail used to originate. It has been extended, however, and now starts at the campground, north of Cañon de Salas in Cañon del Trigo. This is a rugged hike, with lower and upper switchbacks as it winds its way southeast up the mountains. There are many views north and south, and probably this is one of the better trails for seeing the bighorn sheep. The closest connecting trail would be Red Canyon to the north.

Approximate hiking time is five to six hours.

COMANCHE CANYON TRAIL (#182) *8 miles*

This hike also originates in John F. Kennedy Campground, heading north across the foothills to Comanche Canyon. It intersects the Crest Trail four miles north of Capilla Peak where Trail Canyon Trail descends the east side. This is another steep, rugged climb, recommended for backpackers or hard hikers. The trail goes north for several miles out of the campground, passing a stock tank and private land before it turns to begin its ascent up Comanche Canyon. It stays primarily in the canyon bottom, going by several springs, until it starts its climb up the north side of the canyon to its end at the Crest Trail.

Approximate hiking time is five to six hours.

NON-MAINTAINED TRAILS

There are several more trails ascending the west face of the Manzanos; they are unmaintained, very difficult to find, and not recommended for recreational hikers.

Ojito Trail is a five-mile hike up to the junction of Crest Trail and Fourth of July Trail. It begins approximately half a mile west of the Valencia–Torrence County line in Township 7N, Range 4E, Section 25.

Encino Canyon Trail climbs five miles to the Crest Trail several hundred yards south of the junction with Bosque Trail. It

SALAS TRAIL

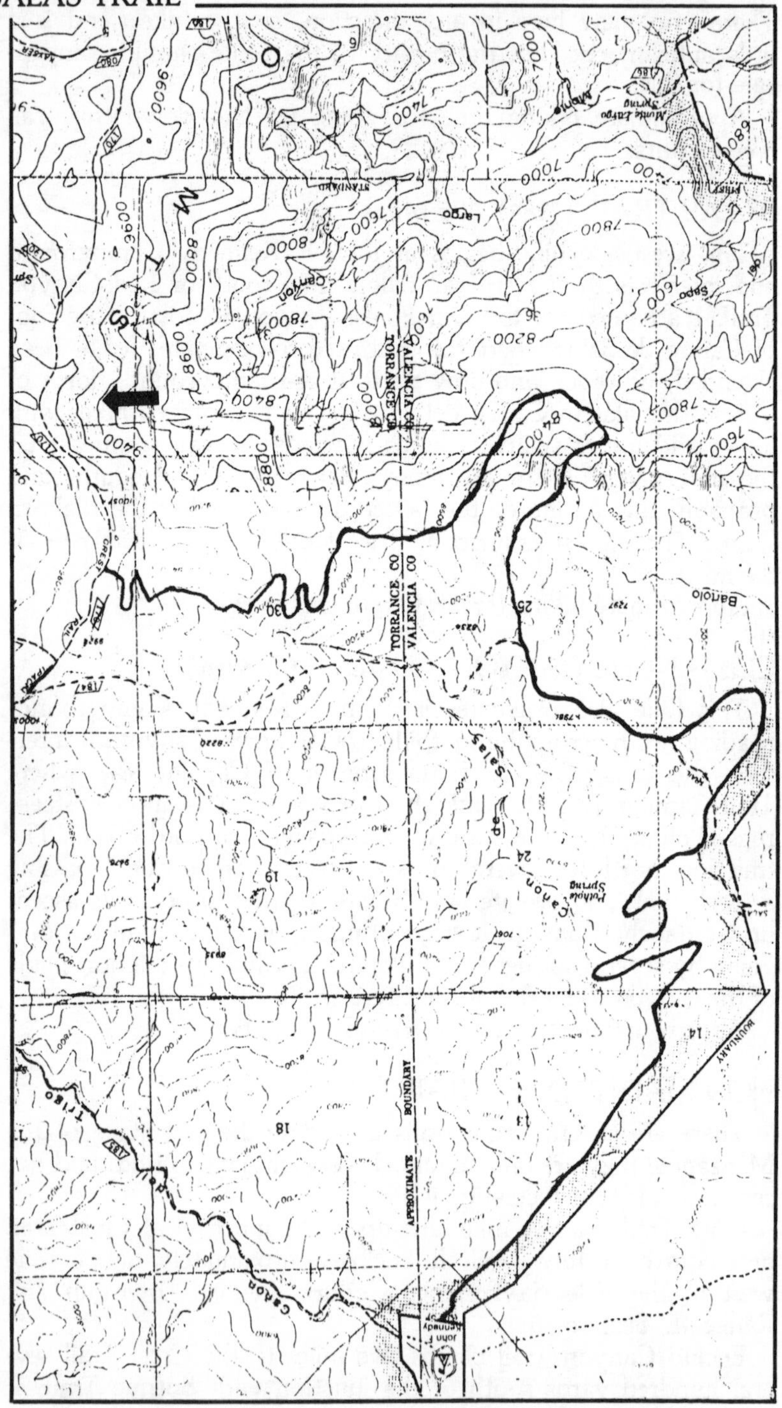

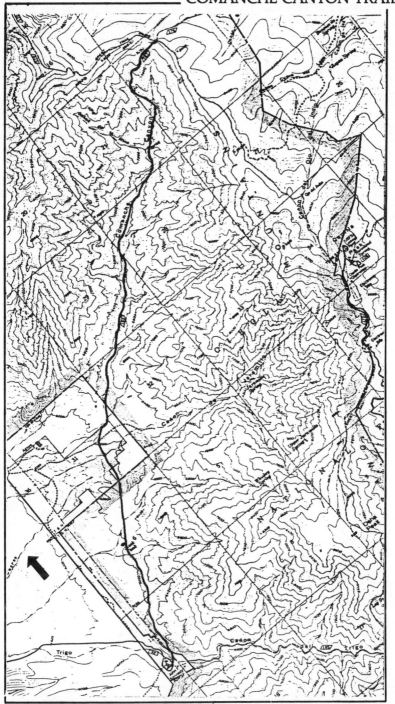

begins at the Valencia–Torrence County line in T 6N, R 5E, S 18.

Monte Largo Trail (#186) is a 5.5-mile climb to the Crest Trail, emerging about a quarter mile north of Manzano Peak. It begins at the Valencia–Torrence County line at Monte Largo Spring in T 4N, R 4E, S 1.

PART IV.
CROSS-COUNTRY SKI TRAILS
IN THE SANDIA MOUNTAINS

Introduction

Cross-country skiing in the Sandias is the best of both worlds—enough easy terrain for the inexperienced skier and lots of steep trails for those seeking the downhill thrill. Until the last few years most cross-country skiers from Albuquerque traveled to the Jemez Mountains or the Sangre de Cristos for their adventures. But now that the Sandia Peak Ski Area offers cross-country lessons and the Forest Service has marked and mapped an elaborate trail system, new skiers are learning in the Sandias and old hands are returning to the local slopes. So far there seems to be enough room for everyone; I've skied many mornings on designated trails without meeting anyone.

In this section I will describe some cross-country trips which, like the hikes in the previous sections, enable one to travel in a loop instead of backtracking the same trail. Most of the trails are included on the excellent Forest Service ski touring map of the Sandias, available at the Sandia Ranger Station and at most mountaineering stores in Albuquerque. The map also rates the trails as to difficulty, and I have included these ratings in my descriptions. For some of these routes mileage figures are not available, and I have not included skiing time because this would vary so much among skiers.

Clothing

If you aren't properly dressed for a day of ski touring, you'll have a miserable trip, so heed these tips and enjoy your day.

It's often hard to predict exactly what the weather portends, so dressing in layers is the safest insurance against heat and cold. I *always* wear thermal underwear, tops and bottoms, no matter how warm a day it looks to be. Most complaints about underwear concern its bulkiness, but if you can spare the money, the best investment is to buy duofold, which fits the body snugly and looks decent even if you strip to your shirt layer on a warm day. It will last you forever, too.

The next layers are more diverse, though they should be made of wool and cotton. A cotton turtleneck keeps the neck warm, covered by a wool sweater for cold weather. Wool pants or knickers with wool knee socks are best for repelling dampness from the inevitable fall in the snow. Most skiers these days also wear gaiters, waterproof coverings that fasten around the lower leg to protect your pants from deep snow. They're not absolutely necessary, especially with knickers or wool pants, but they do come in handy if you're wearing jeans or cords.

I always wear a down (or synthetic) vest, even if the day looks temperate. I can always shed underlayers of shirts if I get too warm, but nothing can compare with the protection of a vest in cold weather. I wear a vest instead of a parka as the sleeveless-ness aids in efficient arm movement and also provides ventilation.

Good footwear is essential. Since most cross-country ski boots are low-cut and roomy, I wear two to three layers of socks, depending on the weather. Next to the skin is a close-fitting cotton sock, over that wool knee socks, and if necessary, on top, a pair of heavy rag socks. Just as your feet need protection, so does your head, where body heat escapes. Wear a wool hat that fits over your ears. And bring along a wool scarf that can wrap your face and neck for extra protection. I always wear sunglasses, or goggles, for eye protection against the snow glare.

Gloves are another essential. In extremely warm weather it's nice to ski bare-handed, but if hands get cold, life is miserable. Insulated, waterproof gloves or mittens are best. Leather gloves with waterproof covers will do, or wool mittens that shed the moisture. They can and do get wet, though.

Day Pack Essentials

We are discussing day ski trips here so I'll limit my pack items to that orientation. Some kind of liquid is called for, preferably hot, but as most skiers don't want to carry around the weight of a thermos, juice, tea, lemonade, or gatorade will suffice. Something with some tang to it is preferable to water on a cold day.

A high-energy lunch helps compensate for the energy spent on the trip. Protein, carbohydrate, and quick-energy sugar replenish your energy stores. Lots of snacks help you keep going through the day.

Sunscreen is essential. The intense rays of the sun will burn any exposed skin (unless well-leathered), so be cautious and apply protective lotion, even on a cloudy day.

If you rent or own non-wax skis, you can ignore this para-graph about waxing, although it's nice to have the knowledge for the day you may end up on waxable skis. Most people I know actually prefer waxable skis and don't let the art of waxing intimidate them. Recently, wax manufacturers have come out with a two-wax system that eliminates the confusion: one wax for new snow, one wax for old, slushy snow. For most day trips in the Sandias these two will suffice. In the spring, when extreme snow conditions call for additional wax, a klister can be added (this gooey stuff comes in a tube and is applied with a stick).

The full range of waxes includes five color-coded waxes ranging from green for extremely cold, dry snow through blue, purple, red, and yellow as the weather warms up and the snow becomes less pristine. A waxing kit usually includes all five waxes (sometimes including a white at the cold end and a klister for spring), a cork for rubbing in the wax, and a scraper for getting it off. Remember when applying wax that the softer wax for older snow can be applied over the harder, cold-condition waxes, but not vice-versa. So always start out with the hardest wax you think you'll need and improvise from there.

Some people include an emergency ski repair kit in their pack, but I don't think it's really necessary for day trips in the Sandias. You can pack a screwdriver for binding emergencies.

Ski Equipment

I won't go into a lengthy discussion on cross-country ski equipment. There are books available on the subject, and salespeople in the mountaineering stores can help you choose the equipment best for you. I *will* say that as in any popular sport, the equipment has become very sophisticated and, consequently, expensive. Keep in mind the type of skiing you will be doing in the Sandias, Jemez, or wherever, and don't over-outfit yourself just because equipment is available.

Cross-country skis were made of wood until the fiberglas industry took over. Wood skis are still available and are perfectly adequate for ski touring trips where the terrain is not too rugged. They break more easily, of course, and don't have the edges for sharp turns and stopping. Fiberglas skis are more durable, and can be equipped with metal edges for more control.

There are several kinds of binding, mostly toe bindings where the heel is free for the necessary cross-country motion. Also available are bindings with lock-in heels for more maneuverability on downhill runs.

Leather boots offer the best support and durability. They can be either low-cut for normal touring or high-cut for mountaineering. Just make sure to wear the kind of socks you will wear out on the slopes when you try them on.

Poles are pretty straightforward, made mostly of fiberglas with leather handgrips and straps. Be sure you are measured correctly for your height when buying them.

Trails

First, a word of warning about car access to trails. During winter weather State Road 44 is often closed to vehicles without snow tires, chains, or four-wheel drive. The snowplows are usually out pretty soon after a snowstorm, however, to clear the road to the Sandia Peak Ski Area and on up to the Crest. Parking can be a problem. Usually the snowplows clear out the Crest parking lots and the roads into Capulin and Nine Mile picnic areas for parking. Unless your car is inside the white lines on the Crest Highway (Forest Road 536), the Bernalillo County Sheriff Department can issue a ticket for obstructing traffic. Since piled-up snow from the plowing usually covers the white lines, it's best not to park along the highway at all. I've tried to describe trips that are accessible from the parking areas.

KIWANIS MEADOW (ROUTE #3)—CREST TRAIL (ROUTE #2)—SERVICE ROAD (ROUTE #1)

This is a good route for a beginner to get the feel of skiing. The loop provides both up-and-down terrain and lots of wide open space to practice stops and turns.

Drive all the way to Sandia Crest to begin the trip. The lower parking area is usually cleared, and at the south end of the lot is the old road leading into Kiwanis Meadow. It's a short, gradual downhill glide to the meadow, perfect for the beginner.

At the meadow, the possibilities are varied. If you stay along the top (west) end and traverse the meadow you meet up with the Crest Trail leading out to Kiwanis Cabin, the stone hut sitting on the edge of the ridge, overlooking the west side. From here the trail follows the ridgeline down toward the trees and across to the Tram. Take some time to ski through the meadow, practicing your stride and maneuvering ability. Several Forest Service cross-country trails emerge into the meadow on the north end, just below the road from the parking lot. We will come back to the Crest on these trails at the end of the tour.

The Crest Trail from Kiwanis Meadow to the Tram has some steep spots and after several days of no snow can be quite crusty from shade and people use. The trail follows the ridgeline south with many overlooks toward the Tram; after turning south it stays in the trees the last half mile to the Tram.

A cup of coffee or hot chocolate at the Tram cafeteria is too good to pass up. On a warm day you can sit out on the terrace and watch the downhill skiers come up on the Tram. Inside, you can eat your sack lunch with no one bothering you.

The route back toward the Crest is the Tram Service Road (in the summertime limited to Tramway and Forest Service employees) running north from the restaurant. You can see the ski area instructors with their cross-country ski classes just to the right (east) of the road. This area gets a lot of use, of course, but it provides the easiest access back to the Crest. The one mile back to the Crest Highway (State Road 536) is mostly uphill (but not too steep). The junction with Route #3, which we will take back to Kiwanis Meadow and the Crest, is just before the gate, which blocks the road in the summertime.

The trail turns left (west) into the trees; a short distance later you come to a left-right junction. To the left the trail climbs a short distance back to Kiwanis Meadow. It emerges at the north end, just below the parking lot road (Route #3), so you must climb back up to the road and north to the Crest. To the right at the junction, the trail winds up and down through the trees until it circles back toward the meadow, meeting up with the left fork of the trail as it emerges into the meadow. Watch for the trail as it circles back south toward the meadow or you will end up at the Crest Highway. This is actually the beginning of another route, Route #4, the Survey Trail, which crosses the highway and continues north toward Cañon del Agua overlook.

At the convergence of the trails at the north end of the meadow there is another trail which turns north and goes back through the trees to the Crest parking lot (it traverses the mountain just below the Kiwanis Meadow road). It is a more difficult trail, however, and should be traveled only by the more experienced skier.

Most of these trails are marked with the Forest Service blue diamonds and come out at either Kiwanis Meadow, the Crest Highway, or the parking lot, so it's pretty hard to get lost. They are usually well traveled, too, so you can follow the many tracks of fellow skiers.

CAPULIN (ROUTE #7)—NINE MILE—
CHALLENGE TRAIL (ROUTE #6)

This route is a little more difficult, with quite a few uphill climbs and downhill stretches, but it's one of the nicest that I've skied.

The trail begins at Capulin Picnic Ground at the north end of the parking lot. There is a Forest Service trail marker visible from the lot. The trail starts out fairly level but soon starts climbing as it makes a big loop around the picnic ground and heads back out to the Crest Highway (State Road 536). Watch for a switchback after the first long ascent; arrows point the way.

Another climb brings you to the top of a short downhill stretch where the trail opens up as it passes through Capulin Canyon. Then it's just a short distance to the Crest Highway, and a scramble over the snowbanks lining the road.

Watch for cars crossing the road; don't assume that they can stop for you on a snow- or ice-packed surface. The trail continues on the south side of the road just a short distance below where you emerged. A Forest Service marker designates the trail, which is actually a little spur of the Route #6 trail which begins at the Tramway Service Road and ends at the bottom of the Sandia Peak Ski Area. Follow the trail to the right as it climbs up to Nine Mile Picnic Ground on the old entrance road (circumvented by the re-routing of the Crest Highway in 1982).

This old road leads to the new road entering the picnic ground. Turn left onto the entry road and follow it into the area. Sometimes it's been plowed, so you'll have to ski along the snowbanks. The picnic ground is a good place to stop for a snack.

Continue around the outhouse to the left, and watch closely for the trail markers in the trees to the left. The trail heads steeply up into the woods to connect with the upper portion of Route #6. It's about a half-mile trip to the main part of the trail; the spur trail meets the main trail in the middle of a stand of firs. Follow the trail markers to the left, down the mountain.

It's all downhill from here. The trail zigzags down the mountain staying relatively close to the highway, although far enough away for one to feel isolated. It's full of great downhill swooshes through the trees; watch for the blazes as it makes its various turns.

The trail opens and levels out for a while, and you can actually hear the skiers on the downhill ski slopes off to the right. Then, as it enters the trees again, watch for glimpses of the Crest Highway to the left. Just before the trail starts a climb up the right along a ridge, leave the trail and ski down to the road only a short distance away. You will emerge onto the Crest Highway just below Capulin Picnic Ground. Cross the road and ski back up to the entrance road along the snowbank. It's a nice level run into the picnic ground.

There's another fun ski run leading out of Capulin Picnic Ground, but it involves a hike back up the mountain to retrieve your car. The trail begins just south of the outhouse in the lower parking area. It runs east, down the mountain, and connects with the lower Capulin Road, which in turn connects with Las

Huertas Canyon Road (State Road 44) just below Balsam Glade Picnic Ground. It's an uninterrupted downhill run (except for the gate where the trail meets the Capulin Road) and not too difficult for a beginner. At the junction with Las Huertas Road it's a short climb up to Balsam Glade and another climb along the Crest Highway back to Capulin. It's easy to catch a ride, though, and the downhill run is worth the effort of getting back.

NORTH CREST (ROUTE #2)—10K (ROUTE #5)— UPPER ROAD CUT *approximately 4.5 miles*

This ski loop is basically the same route as the hike described in Part II, Section 1, except that the last leg of the return is along the roadcut rather than 10K Trail. It's a fairly arduous trip, and recommended for the more experienced skier.

Leave your car at the Crest parking lot. The trip begins along North Crest Trail, easily followed by the old Forest Service blazes in the trees (there are no blue cross-country markers). Where the trail follows the ridgeline there are spectacular winter-wonderland views of the west face of the mountains. Several long, fun downhills carry you through the trees before the trail levels out a little before emerging into the meadow at Cañon del Agua overlook. In a good snow year you may have trouble finding the rock bench overlooking the canyon.

The descent along 10K Trail to the uppermost road cut is labeled most difficult by the cross-country sign system. The trail begins off to the right just as you emerge from the trees into the Cañon del Agua clearing. You'll probably end up negotiating some of it sitting down, but it's only a short distance to the road-cut. The trail is easily followed, marked all the way with blue blazes.

10K Trail continues on down across the roadcut toward Cañon Media Spring and out onto Crest Highway (State Road 536). It's a difficult trail on skis, so I choose to return to the highway by way of the roadcut. It's an up-and-down excursion (mostly up) as it traverses the side of the mountain. There's lots of room to practice turns here, coming down off numerous hills.

Stay to the right when the roadcut forks, and you'll come out higher up on the road across from the continuing roadcut on the south side of the highway (also fun to ski). It's easy to hitch a ride back up to the Crest, or if you have some energy reserves, it's not that far to ski on up. You can connect with Route #6 on the south side of the highway, following the roadcut to the junction of the trail, or ski alongside the Crest Highway to the Crest.

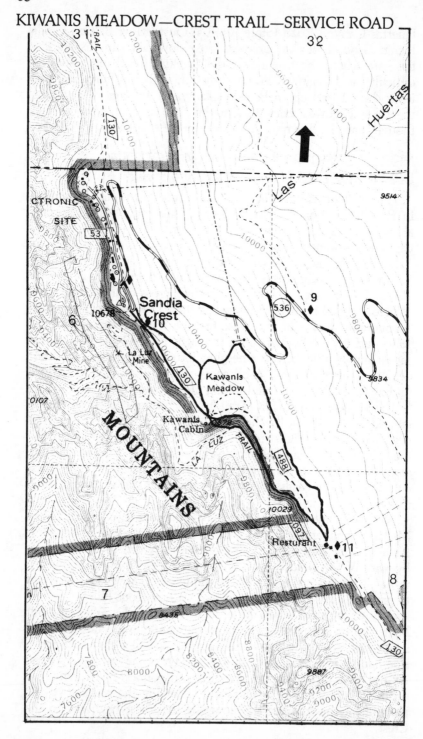

CAPULIN—NINE MILE—CHALLENGE TRAIL

10K (ROUTE #5)—TREE SPRING (ROUTE #8) *4 miles*

This route follows the southern part of 10K Trail over to Tree Spring Trail, and is recommended for the experienced skier. 10K is marked most difficult, and parts of Tree Spring are steep.

The tour begins off the Crest Highway (State Road 536) where 10K Trail heads south toward the ski basin (3.5 miles from the junction of the Crest Highway and State Road 44). Blue cross-country blazes designate the trail. Unless the snow has been cleared to the inside of the white line it is illegal to park on the highway, so you can either park your car at the bottom of Tree Spring Trail and catch a ride up to the trailhead, or have a friend drop you off. You can ski this route the opposite way, from Tree Spring to 10K, but it's almost all uphill and a lot more work.

The first part of the trail is some easy up and down, and a beautiful forest trip. About half a mile in you reach the first of the Sandia Peak ski slopes. 10K is blazed on both sides of the slopes as the trail works its way across the ski area, but sometimes the markers are not immediately obvious. Stay on a pretty steady traversing course. And watch out for downhill skiers!

After eight crossings you're back in the trees for good. The last time I skied 10K there were no blue blazes marking the route once it leaves the ski area heading south, so be careful to stay on the trail. If the snow is not too deep, the old Forest Service tree blazes are visible. Almost immediately into the trees the trail begins a descent of Cañon Madera, then meets a gentler climb back out up through a stand of oak. This is an easy place to lose the trail; stay in the oak as you head southwest until the trail becomes more obvious as views of the east side open up.

10K Trail ends at the junction of Tree Spring and South Crest Trails. It's a two-mile downhill swoosh along Tree Spring to SR 44. It's mostly a gentle descent, but there are a few steep hills and some precipitous drops.

CHALLENGE TRAIL (ROUTE #6) *4.3 miles*

This downhill run from the Tram Service Road to the Sandia Peak Ski Area includes many steep pitches, so this tour is recommended for the experienced skier seeking some downhill thrills.

The trail begins just south of the gate on the Service Road. If there is no room to park on the Crest Highway (State Road 536), you can add some mileage to your trip by parking at the Crest and coming down through Kiwanis Meadow to the Service Road. You'll have to arrange for someone to pick you up at the ski area base or catch a ride back up to the Crest. If you want to avoid transportation problems entirely, drive to the ski basin, buy a one-way ticket on the chairlift, and ski back down to your car (the ski area requires that you have some sort of safety line from your ski to boot or leg).

Route #6 basically follows the Crest Highway until it reaches the roadcuts, which are suitable for skiing back over to the road if you wish to keep your trip short. The longer roadcut is blazed (ski down through the opening until you pick up the blazes heading north) and is actually just a spur of the #6 trail as it meets up with 10K Trail following the Crest Highway downhill to the 10K turn south toward the ski area. Route #6 continues down the mountain from its junction with 10K, in and out along the road, until the junction with the spur trail leading to Nine Mile Picnic Ground (described on page 21). Stay to the right to continue on #6; there are several steep pitches and a meadow to traverse before the trail emerges at the road right below the entrance to Capulin Picnic Ground. The trail continues back into the trees and levels out considerably as it heads toward the junction with State Road 44. It then swings around to the south to follow the line of the highway to the ski basin. The last leg follows an old ski basin road uphill before emerging near the poma lift at the north end of the ski area.

The blazes on the Challenge Trail are spaced fairly far apart, so be sure to watch closely as the trail makes its turns and switches down the mountain. The ski patrol almost always makes a run down this trail first thing in the morning so their ski tracks will make the route easier to follow. Allow yourself at least four hours to make this route a pleasant experience instead of a ski race down the mountain.

KIWANIS MEADOW (ROUTE #3)—SURVEY TRAIL (ROUTE #4)—NORTH CREST TRAIL (ROUTE #2)

Save this excursion until you are truly a proficient skier. When you are able to ski it, though, it's quite an adventure.

The loop begins easily enough along Route #3 to Kiwanis Meadow south from the Crest parking lot. At the end of the downhill run to the north end of the meadow, turn east across the meadow to where the Forest Service trails enter the trees, heading back north. Take the trail to the right, traveling northeast through the trees. This whole system of trails is described in Section 1. For our purposes, stay straight on this trail, following the blue blazes, until it emerges next to the Crest Highway (State Road 536) and continues in and out of the trees alongside the road. Eventually it comes to an end at the highway. Look directly across the road to the north side and you can see the blue blazes marking the Survey Trail.

The Survey Trail is marked most difficult by the Forest Service. The first part of the trail is indeed so, with several steep pitches (both up and down) initiating the skier into the difficult route. The entire trail is blazed, but the markers are few and far between, so follow them carefully. Several trees have fallen across the trail, and in many places the path is quite narrow, so use caution in your downhill glides to avoid wrapping around a tree.

After several steep ascents the trail passes under the power line and begins to traverse north across the mountain. The Forest Service map says it's 1.6 miles to the intersection with 10K Trail, just below Cañon del Agua overlook, but it seems longer. It's a beautiful trail, though, offering long glides through the trees, almost all downhill. Most of the difficult sections are found along the first half of the trail, so the second half provides needed respite before the ascent back along North Crest Trail.

The Survey Trail emerges at the 10K Trail about 50 yards below Cañon del Agua overlook. You're at the bottom of one of the steep   pitches on the 10K, so if the snow is packed down enough, I recommend removing your skis and hiking up to the meadow (to the left). Then you can clear off a place to sit on the stone wall (if you can find it) and enjoy the view of the Rio Grande valley before the trip back to the Crest.

North Crest Trail (route #2) is described on page 25; this route ascends the trail rather than allowing you to enjoy it. downhill, but it's not all that far to the Crest (about two miles) and it's a relatively easy climb. The trail heads south just to the left of where 10K Trail emerges at the Cañon del Agua clearing. There are no blue blazes on the trees, but you should be able to follow the old Forest Service hatchet marks (and the trail is almost always worn down by other skiers unless you're traveling in new snow). It basically follows the ridgeline south, up the mountain past North Peak to the Crest. There are magnificent overlooks along the entire route; you can see the Needle, the Prow, and Chimney Canyon. Although almost all the trail is uphill, there are several sections where you can rest your bones with some downhill glides. After a last long uphill climb, the trail levels out to the left, just below the end of the radio tower road, and traverses the last half mile beneath the road. The trail ends at the Crest Highway, just opposite the lower Crest parking lot.

Because of the difficulty of the Survey Trail and the ascent of North Crest Trail, allow yourself most of the day for this trip.

PART V.
CROSS-COUNTRY SKI TRAILS
IN THE MANZANO MOUNTAINS

There are no designated cross-country ski trails in the Man-zanos, but there are several areas suitable for skiing when there's sufficient snow. I will describe three areas on the east side of the mountain, accessible from South 14.

FOREST ROAD 55 FROM TAJIQUE TO FOURTH OF JULY CAMPGROUND

According to the Forest Service, Forest Road 55 out of Tajique is snowplowed to the Enlow Youth Camp during inclement weather. From there to Fourth of July Campground the road makes a good cross-country run, and on into the campground as well. You can also continue along FR 55 toward Torreón, using some of the old logging roads that detour off the main road. The trails which intersect FR 55—Fourth of July, Cerro Blanco, Bosque, and Trail Canyon—are really too steep for good cross-country skiing, although the truly hardy ski tourer could use them for access to the Manzano Crest Trail.

RED CANYON CAMPGROUND

Forest Road 235 out of Manzano to Red Canyon Campground is not maintained during the winter, but if you can get close to the campground the series of logging roads off Forest Road 422 provide some good cross-country skiing.

There are several routes you can follow off FR 422. In Part III, Section 3, I give directions for FR 422 and the turn to Ox Canyon Trail; you can ski from the turn to the junction of the "Primitive Road" and then turn right, instead of left toward the trailhead. This will take you in a loop back to FR 253. If you turn left, toward the trailhead, it's an easy cross-country tour to the junc-tion of a logging road turning left (south). This road eventually leads back to FR 422, and you can ski back (north) along FR 422 to FR 253.

Beyond these loops FR 422 continues several miles south to the junction of Forest Road 275, which leads to Kayser Mill Trail and provides additional skiing routes along connecting logging roads. This is a long way from FR 253, however, so unless you drive farther south along FR 422, these roads are too far away for a comfortable day's skiing.

NEW CANYON (FOREST ROAD 245)

Forest Road 245 out of Manzano to New Canyon Camp-ground and Capilla Peak is also not maintained during the win-ter, but if you can make it to the campground there's an old logging road to the north that can be used as a ski trail. The rest of the way to Capilla Peak is all uphill, of course, but it's a beautiful trip in the wintertime. If you do make it all the way to the top, Capilla Peak Campground offers a loop road for skiing. I wouldn't recommend the Manzano Crest Trail either north or south, as there are many precipitous sections in both directions.